HER BEST DEFENSE

By

Cordell Parvin

First trade paperback edition

2022 Copyright © 2022 by Cordell Parvin

All rights reserved. No part of this publication may be reproduced, distributed, or transmitted in any form or by any means, including photocopying, recording, or other electronic or mechanical methods, without the prior written permission of the publisher, except in the case of fair use involving brief quotations embodied in critical reviews and certain other uses permitted by copyright law. Permission requests should be sent to the author.

ISBN: 979-8-218-06317-7

DEDICATION

I want to dedicate the book to my wife, Nancy and my daughter, Jill. They took care of me in 2022 when I was sick and could not take care of myself.

ACKNOWLEDGEMENTS

I would like to acknowledge Jeff Kravitz, Bob Burleson, Jaimie Field and Bill Lynch. Each person took time to read what I had written and provide feedback.

ABOUT THE AUTHOR

Cordell Parvin practiced law for 38 years and then coached, mentored and taught young lawyers. His novels focus on courtroom dramas and are torn in part from actual cases

November 2019 to January 2020

CHAPTER 1

Gabriela

As Daniel and I walked out of my townhome on our way to a romantic dinner, I looked down at my cell phone and saw the message from Father Michael. I read the message because I did not want Daniel to hear it.

"Gabriela, this is Father Michael. Emma Riley needs your help. Her seventeen-year-old daughter may have shot and killed a prominent Dallas businessman. Emma wants you to be her daughter's lawyer. I will fill you in further after nine-thirty Mass tomorrow."

By the fall and early winter of 2019, I had tried two high-profile cases I had to win to advance my career and reputation. I had dealt with the stress seven days a week and twenty-four hours a day. I welcomed a break after those two exhausting trials, and I was determined not to accept any more high-profile cases. I had planned to begin 2020 by taking it easy and working on my health and fitness.

Thirty minutes later, Daniel and I arrived at The Mansion Restaurant at Turtle Creek. Soon after we were seated, I saw Christopher Duval approaching our table. I froze as Christopher greeted Daniel, leaned down, kissed my cheek, and touched my bare back.

I wiped my cheek and shifted my chair closer to the table to get away from Christopher's hand.

"No need to introduce the two of you," Daniel said sarcastically. "I'm sure you got to know each other when Gabriela defended Sparks."

"Yes. Sparks will forever be grateful. Gabriela saved him from a jury conviction when she saw how the Assistant U.S. Attorney was using social media tricks to manipulate the jury. None of the high-powered consultants Sparks hired put those pieces together."

That was one of the nicer things Christopher had ever said to me. When I was young, I discovered I could see patterns in things others missed. I thought it was a gift at the time and then I later learned that with the gift came a weakness: I was impatient, and I hated details. My attention span was short. Thankfully, I knew of the weakness when I started trying cases, and my father had been my cocounsel for that reason.

I had not had a good experience with Christopher. When I defended his billionaire father, Christopher had been married, but that had not stopped him from setting me up on a trip to Houston during the Oil and Gas Conference. He invited me to join his father and him for dinner at a well-known Houston restaurant. When I arrived, he was alone and planning on spending the night with me. I spent the evening telling him no in every way I could.

Christopher was a seduction artist. He did it by making lingering eye contact. I figured he had come to the Mansion to make a play for one or more of the single women seated at the bar.

He was so full of himself that he either couldn't figure out that Daniel and I wanted to be alone, or he didn't care. He pulled a chair away from another table and sat at ours. "Gabriela, you look stunning as always," Christopher said. "You're dressed to the nines as always. Gorgeous."

I raised my left eyebrow, hoping Christopher would see my disapproval and leave us alone. He missed my signal and continued. "Daniel, you're quite the lucky one to be dining with one of the most beautiful women in Dallas."

I shook my head and Daniel sighed. "You haven't changed since we were in high school," he said.

"I'm just being honest." The waiter slid past him to deliver drinks to me and Daniel. "Did you hear? Henry Esposito was shot and killed?"

"What?" Daniel asked.

"They say two teenage girls robbed him, killed him, and then stole his BMW."

"Two teenage girls robbed and killed Henry. How did they get into his apartment?" Daniel asked.

"Good question." Christopher glanced over at Daniel. He and Daniel clearly knew more than they were letting on.

Damn. Now I knew why I received the voicemail from Father Michael. I also remembered that Daniel had introduced me to Esposito at a law firm picnic during the summer. I had caught him staring at me like I was going to be his next lay.

I was already thinking of reasons I could tell Father Michael to persuade him and Emma Riley to find another lawyer to represent the teenage girl. Yet, I wanted to defend the girl to Daniel and Christopher.

"I bet he was abusing the girls," I said. "And that they didn't just show up to kill him and take his car. In Texas, there is a defense when a person makes unwanted sexual advances."

Christopher looked at Daniel with a fake grin. He knew exactly what his friend had been doing in the apartment.

Before I could challenge him, Christopher said, "I'll leave the two of you to dine. Sanchez, I'll tell Sparks I saw you. I'm sure he will be happy to hear you are doing well and seeing Daniel."

***

I woke up first on Sunday morning, got out of bed, and put on Daniel's white shirt that I found on the floor. I hadn't slept well.

I had worried about what I could tell Father Michael after Mass, and I had been uneasy being around Christopher again.

I had drunk too many lemon-drop martinis and too much wine afterward. Even then, I couldn't stop thinking about Daniel's close friendship with Christopher Duval and what they knew about Henry Esposito.

When I walked through the living room toward the kitchen, I saw my black dress, heels, and underwear on the floor near the couch. Two empty wine glasses and an empty bottle of Caymus Vineyards Cabernet Sauvignon were on the table.

"You look awesome," Daniel had said as I'd unbuttoned his shirt. By the time we had gotten to my bedroom, we were both naked, embracing and kissing each other. I remembered pushing Daniel onto my bed and climbing on top of him. Each time Daniel got close, I stopped him. Finally, I started pulsating. He gasped, and I knew he couldn't hold his climax back any longer. Afterward, Daniel lay there exhausted, with a big smile. I had worn him out.

In the kitchen I turned my attention back to my Keurig coffee maker, inserted a capsule, and watched as it filled my cup. I put in a second capsule for Danial and added Splenda as it dripped.

I drank from my cup and brought the second to the bedroom for Daniel, who opened his eyes, then sat up in bed. "You look sexy in that shirt and your bare bottom," he said.

He pulled on my arm. After giving him a subtle wink, I started to walk away. I enjoy flirting, but I had no time for it that morning.

"I had too much to drink last night," I said.

"You're more fun when you've been drinking. Don't you want to make love to me again?"

More fun? Was he right? Was that all he cared about? I didn't even like myself when I was drinking.

"Daniel, it's six-thirty in the morning, and I'm going out for a run and then go to Mass."

"It's Sunday. Can't you skip the run this one time?"

He got out of bed naked, came over to me, unbuttoned his shirt, and put his hand inside. I stepped back.

"Daniel, I told you I don't have time. I need to go for a run before mass." Putting on my best sly grin, I added, "Besides, you will have to do a lot more to earn what you are asking for at six-thirty in the morning."

He asked what he needed to do.

"That is for you to think about and figure out," I replied.

After the Sunday Mass, Father Michael stopped me as I walked to my car. "Gabriela, as I told you in the voicemail, Emma Riley's daughter needs your help."

I tried to place Emma Riley, and her daughter, and thought about the last time Father Michael asked for my help. He had asked me to represent unaccompanied immigrant children who had gone through hell to get to this country and were facing deportation. I had felt lots of pressure because of how important it was for me to win and keep the children here.

"In the voicemail, you said Emma Riley's daughter may have shot a prominent businessman. Can you tell me more?" I asked.

"Her seventeen-year-old daughter, Hope, and her friend shot and killed Henry Esposito, a prominent Dallas investment banker, stole his car and headed for Miami. I understand the Dallas police plan to charge her with murder. Emma Riley and I want you to represent Hope."

I wanted to start telling him why I was not the right lawyer to defend Hope, but a group of parishioners had gathered around him.

"Let's talk tomorrow," he said.

Damn!

Chapter 2

Gabriela

On Monday, I entered the U.S. Federal Court House in Dallas to represent Wayne Robertson. He was a real estate investor who had purchased property along interstate highways and resold it at exorbitant prices to the Texas Department of Transportation.

Robertson, the grown son of one of my Parker and McEvoy partners, had pled guilty to fraud after it was clear he had provided bogus valuation information to TxDOT. On that day, Judge Comstock sentenced Robertson to serve thirty months in federal prison and pay one million dollars as restitution to the Texas Department of Transportation. I was glad to be finished with my partner's spoiled brat, narcissistic son. I looked forward to having no court appearances until after the holidays.

Before I drove back to the office, I sat in my car and called Father Michael. I had some questions.

"How did Mrs. Riley learn Hope and Amber had shot Henry Esposito?"

"Hope called her mother from the car as they passed through Shreveport. Emma said Hope was hysterical. She was crying and was very upset. Hope said she and Amber had shot a rich man, and they were driving to Miami to get away."

Many fugitives flee the state where they committed a crime, hoping that the state won't request that they be extradited. How would two teenage girls know that? In Texas, some people believed "he deserved to die," was a valid defense. If Henry Esposito was a predator, would Texas seek to extradite the girls?

"If they make it to Miami, Texas may never bring them back," I said.

"They didn't make it to Miami," Father Michael said. "The police arrested them in Baton Rouge, and they are holding the girls in the Baton Rouge Jail."

"Texas must request they be extradited, and the Louisiana governor must sign an order to extradite them to Dallas. Has our governor requested extradition?"

"I don't know. I called because Emma Riley wants you to represent Hope."

"Does she want me to fight the extradition in Louisiana? She needs a Louisiana lawyer to do that."

"No, her mother wants her to come home. She believes when you tell the district attorney what happened, they will drop the charges."

I still thought I was not the right lawyer to take on Hope's defense. I hadn't defended anyone, much less a juvenile in a Dallas County criminal case. I also knew I would have to fight the powers in my law firm because Emma Riley had no money to pay. I quickly thought of a response.

"Father, I don't have the right experience, and my law firm will not let me take on a murder case with no expectation of being paid."

"You have the experience. You've represented criminal defendants in some of the most publicized cases in Dallas."

Damn, he doesn't understand what he is asking me to do.

"Father, those were white-collar criminal cases in federal court. I've never defended a homicide defendant, and I've never defended a juvenile. I don't have any contacts in the DA's office. There are far more experienced lawyers in Dallas who would be better suited to defend Hope."

"Gabriela, Mrs. Riley specifically asked for you to defend Hope. She believes you are the only one who will care enough to help Hope. If you don't represent Hope, she'll be stuck with a public defender. You can't let that happen."

I knew Mrs. Riley could not afford to pay our firm or an experienced criminal lawyer. Father Michael had ignored that point.

"Father, sometimes having a lawyer who cares enough is a disadvantage, not an advantage. Hope needs a lawyer who specializes in defending juveniles in state court."

"Caring about what happens to Hope is more important than experience representing juveniles in state court. Will you at least meet with Mrs. Riley?"

I sighed, knowing there was no argument I could make that would persuade the priest. He knew how much I didn't want to take this case and it didn't matter to him. Father Michael was not going to let me say no. Trials are stressful. I had successfully dealt with the stress many times. But I started stressing more over jumping into what had previously been unchartered waters with a teenage girl's future at stake.

I was stuck. I would face our managing partner's wrath. The only saving grace was that I expected the trial to be finished in a few months.

"You can set up a meeting tomorrow morning. But I want you to know I plan to persuade Emma Riley to hire a lawyer experienced defending juveniles accused of serious crimes."

Chapter 3

Gabriela

I am far more comfortable being a specialist who knows a lot about a little than I am being a generalist who knows a little about a lot. As a result, I rarely venture into unchartered territory like the Dallas County courts. I tossed and turned all night, trying to think of more ways to persuade Father Michael to find another lawyer. He knew that if I didn't defend Hope, a public defender would defend her. At the very least, the public defender would have experience in the Dallas County courts, and he or she would know the judges and the prosecutors.

Unfortunately, I knew that could not persuade him. So, I had to make one of two bad choices. Either I could agree to represent a teenage girl in another high-profile case, in a court where I had no experience, and face the wrath of my entire law firm, or I would have to face Emma Riley, who Father Michael had convinced that I was the only lawyer who could represent Hope.

I wasn't sure I could learn all the things I didn't know in time to defend Hope. I was afraid to take the case. I knew a teenage girl's future would depend on me convincing a jury she was innocent.

Even so, I wanted to learn more about Henry Esposito. I did a Google search and discovered Esposito had been thirty-nine years old. He had graduated from the same elite private high school as Daniel and Christopher. He was a University of Texas grad and a Penn Business School grad.

I looked at several photos of Esposito. He was a good-looking guy. His eyes were copper colored. His skin was tan like the skin of a famous old-time actor whose name I could not remember. It didn't look natural, so I thought Esposito had likely spent time in a tanning booth.

He was smiling in each photo, with gleaming white teeth. His hair was brown and stylish. He had a manly appearance, suggesting he worked out regularly and was physically fit. I could see why he appealed to women. But I found it hard to picture why a teenager would be interested in him.

There were several photos of Esposito with the rich and famous in Dallas, including athletes, entertainers, politicians, and the well-known elite, including Daniel and Christopher. I thought about which of those high-powered men were on the Esposito party list. He obviously had connections with important people, including the man

I was seriously dating. That added one more excuse for me to bail out before the start of this case.

Esposito and his wife Darla had split a year ago in a messy divorce and brutal custody battle that made the local papers and news. The court record had been sealed, but there were many articles about the contentious divorce. During the two-year divorce proceedings, Esposito had accused his wife of having an affair with the tennis pro at their swanky Dallas country club, and Darla had accused Esposito of having several sexual relationships with high-end prostitutes and his own employees.

One of Daniel's partners had represented Esposito and had employed every divorce lawyer trick to protect his client. During the trial, Darla's lawyer had argued Esposito had been hiding assets. Before he called Esposito's accountant as a witness, the parties settled the case.

Esposito gave Darla their house and custody of their two children seventy percent of the time. He kept his collection of sports cars, a private jet, and homes in Aspen and San Diego.

Prior to meeting Esposito and having children, Darla had a career of her own. She was a well-known women's empowerment speaker, seminar leader, and coach. I learned that Darla used hypnosis and neuro-linguistic programming, known as NLP, to help promote change and empower her clients.

I did some research to better understand NLP. I learned that neuro-linguistic programming was developed by Richard Bandler and John Grinder, who believed it was possible to identify the patterns of thoughts and behaviors of successful individuals and to teach them to others. I found an article Darla had published years ago about NLP.

It turned out that Darla was the one who had connections and had introduced her husband to the rich and powerful Dallas men who later became his clients. In the divorce proceedings, she had argued that Henry owed his success and wealth to her making the introductions.

After Henry and Darla had children, she gave up her career and became more of a philanthropist, devoting her time to helping underprivileged– girls.

I saw photos of Henry and Darla Esposito at charity balls wearing stylish tuxedos and gowns, western wear, and costumes. Darla, who was known as Darlie, was active in at least a dozen well-known charities.

Looking at the photos of Darla, I saw a physically fit, attractive-looking blond, which made me question why Esposito was more interested in teenage girls. He may have found underage girls more easily impressed by his wealth, plane, and cars and manipulated them into sex with him and his friends. I also thought he was the kind of man who felt inadequate with Darla, who had her own successful career and had made a huge contribution to his career.

During the divorce, a reporter had asked Darla how she had met Esposito. Darla had declined to answer, responding that it was personal and private. It likely had nothing to do with his death, but I was surprised by her refusal to answer. What was Darla hiding and why?

I couldn't even count all the reasons I still did not want to take on defending Hope. I had rehearsed how I would gently convey that message to Mrs. Riley. I planned to tell her I didn't have the right experience, which was certainly true.

Chapter 4

Gabriela

At 9:30 the next morning, I walked into Parker & McEvoy's Adams conference room on the thirty-seventh floor and greeted Father Michael. He introduced me to Emma Riley, who appeared to be very uncomfortable in the fancy downtown office setting. I immediately remembered Emma Riley from a Bible study class we had taken together.

Emma Riley was about my age, slightly overweight, with curly black hair that she pulled back. She was doing her best to hold back tears. She wore her gray uniform dress with "Summerset Hotel" stitched on the pocket. Father Michael had told me Emma Riley worked two jobs to take care of Hope and help pay for her voice and acting lessons.

Emma Riley got up from her chair and hugged me.

When they sat down, I asked, "Mrs. Riley, may I get you something to drink?" I pointed to the drinks laid out on the credenza.

"No, Ms. Sanchez."

I spent the next fifteen-minutes explaining why I was not the right lawyer to represent Hope. As I had planned, I told Mrs. Riley that I had never defended a client in Dallas County Court, I had never represented a juvenile, and I didn't know any of the prosecutors. She listened, but to each reason, she looked in my eyes and said, "Please Ms. Sanchez, I know you will help Hope. She and I need you."

I finally agreed I would at least go to Baton Rouge to advise Hope not to say anything to anyone, including her friend. I explained that when the police brought Hope back to Dallas, I would help Emma find a lawyer for her. Before I met with Hope, I wanted to know more.

"May I ask you some questions?" I asked.

"Certainly."

"What can you tell me about Hope?"

Emma Riley looked down at the floor and wiped a tear from her eye. "Hope just turned seventeen. She's a top student, a talented singer and dancer who dreams of a modeling career leading to a career in Hollywood or on Broadway. People have told me that Hope has the talent and the looks to get there. I've worked hard to pay for acting and voice lessons. She's never been in any kind of trouble at school or otherwise. She loves being on stage and performing."

"When you say she loves being on stage and performing, what do you mean?"

"She has dreams of becoming a star. She gets excited when anyone tells her she has talent."

"What can you tell me about her father?"

"She's never met her father. I gave birth to Hope when I was in high school. The man who got me pregnant never acknowledged he was her father. With no father, Hope needs a man her father's age to let her know she is special."

Emma essentially told me that Hope seeks validation from men her father's age, like Henry Esposito.

"Mrs. Riley, do you know how Hope met Henry Esposito?"

"Hope goes to a special high school focused on the performing and visual arts. She sings and acts. Mr. Esposito has contributed a substantial amount of money to the school. He judged the school's annual talent show last year. When Hope came home, she showed me Mr. Esposito's business card and told me he had some contacts in the modeling business and in show business and that he would help her connect with those people."

Did he have more in mind right from the beginning, or was he legitimately trying to help? I would never know for sure. What about Hope? Was she seeking more of his attention right from the beginning? Based on his promises to help her, she likely wanted to get as much as she could from Esposito.

"A few weeks later, Hope started coming home with money, new clothes, and a smart phone, smart watch, and tablet. I asked her where she got the money and the mobile devices. Hope told me she had been modeling and used the money she earned to buy the devices."

"What did you think about Henry Esposito getting Hope modeling opportunities?"

"Hope was excited, so I was excited for her. But Hope hadn't shown me any of her modeling photos. I told her I wanted to meet Mr. Esposito."

I understood why Hope didn't show her mother any of the photos. They were modeling photos, but not the kind to show your mother.

Emma glanced at the ceiling. Then she continued.

"Hope and I met with Henry Esposito at his office. Mr. Esposito was quite gracious. He told me Hope was one of the most talented young girls he had ever seen. Then Mr. Esposito told me he had gotten Hope a role in a local musical and helped her get parts in a television show and a movie filmed here in Dallas.

"Then what happened?" I asked.

"All of a sudden, Hope became distant from me and started questioning anything I told her. She changed. If something I told her conflicted with what Mr. Esposito told her, she treated me like I didn't know anything about her future career."

I became very suspicious when the police came by our apartment and asked to speak to Hope about Mr. Esposito. A girl's mother had called the police and reported that a man in his forties was having sex with her sixteen-year-old daughter. I asked how they got Hope's name and they wouldn't tell me. When they visited the next day, they asked Hope if Mr. Esposito had ever done anything inappropriate to her. Hope said no, but I knew she was holding something back.

Emma shook her head. I thought she would begin crying, but she didn't.

"I asked her after the police had left and she told me Mr. Esposito treated her like a daughter and she appreciated all the help he had given her."

"When Hope called me from the road after Esposito was shot, I was puzzled," Emma continued. "Hope knew the police were investigating Henry Esposito for running a network of teenage girls having sex with him and his friends. I didn't understand why Hope claimed that she and Amber took Esposito's BMW and fled the scene because they didn't think anyone would believe them."

"Mrs. Riley, was Henry Esposito having sex with your daughter?" I knew the answer, but I wanted to see if Emma Riley acknowledged now what had been going on before the shooting.

"At first, I didn't know. I suspected Mr. Esposito was exploiting Hope, but I didn't confront him. I know it sounds stupid now, but at the time, Hope was happy, and I didn't want to ruin that."

I understood why Mrs. Riley didn't want to know the truth. If I had a daughter in the same situation it would have been hard to confront my daughter.

"As soon as the police left, Hope called someone," Emma said.

"Who did she call?"

"I don't know."

Mrs. Riley's face was red and I saw tears in her eyes.

"Father Michael told me Hope called you from the road."

"Yes."

"What did she tell you?"

"Hope was hysterical. She was crying and I could tell she was having a panic attack."

"What did Hope say?"

"Hope said Mr. Esposito had invited them over to his apartment to celebrate her seventeenth birthday and that he had been taking photos and shooting video of them. Then she told me she could not remember anything until she heard the first shot. Hope said she and Amber had shot Mr. Esposito and they were running to Miami to get away."

I made a note on my computer: *Hope didn't shoot Esposito. She had heard Amber's first shot.*

"What else did she say?"

"I could barely understand her. I asked why she and Amber had a pistol. She said Mr. Esposito gave Amber the gun and had taken photos and shot video of her with the gun. At one point I heard Amber say she had shot Mr. Esposito in self-defense. Hope didn't add anything to what Amber said."

"Father Michael said you told Hope you planned to call the police."

"Yes, I told her she and Amber needed to come back home right away to avoid getting in more trouble. I heard Amber say that

Mr. Esposito deserved to die because he was molesting them, but they did not intend to turn around and come home."

"Okay, Mrs. Riley. It is extremely important that Hope not speak to anyone, including Amber. Make sure she knows that."

"She won't speak to anyone, including Amber."

"Is there anything else you can tell me about Hope?"

"She has a Circadian rhythm sleep disorder. She's fallen asleep in class. She also has frequent nightmares, which the doctor told me results from stress and anxiety. I am telling you this because when you meet with her, she could easily be tired, irritable, and given the circumstances, she will most definitely be anxious."

Emma Riley burst into tears again. She pleaded. "My baby, my baby. She's a good girl. You must save her, Ms. Sanchez. Please help my daughter go free."

I didn't know how to respond to the distraught mother. Unlike many sex-trafficking victims, Hope wasn't a teenager who had run away from home into the arms of a pimp who found her on the street, gave her drugs, and sold her online to men looking for sex. Hope had a good life at home with a loving mother.

Why did she let Esposito take advantage of her? I bet it was his promise to help her find a modeling or acting career. I could understand why that promise enticed her. He also paid attention to her. He engaged in conversations and encouraged her to dream big dreams. All of those engagements created a relationship Hope had not experienced before.

As a trial lawyer I learned early on that I would face pressure to win in each case. When I defended Sparks Duval, I was told my career was on the line. If I didn't win, no client would ever hire me again. I dealt with that pressure in part because what other choice did I have? This was different. When I looked at Mrs. Riley, I knew her entire life revolved around her faith and her daughter. If I agreed to defend a teenage girl whose future life would depend on me, the pressure to successfully defend her would be far, far greater than I had experienced before.

Chapter 5

Gabriela

That afternoon, my cell phone rang. I expected the call to be from Father Michael following up on our meeting. I looked and saw the caller ID was congressman Luis Moreno. I took his call.

Moreno was a legend. He was first elected to the House of Representatives in 1980 and had served for the last forty years. He was born and raised in the Valley and was President and CEO of a Mexican food company his father had founded, known for its salsa and other Mexican spices. As a congressman, Moreno focused on helping low-income Americans get access to an excellent education and helping those individuals start their own minority-owned businesses.

I would not be a lawyer without Congressman Moreno's help. He had written a letter of recommendation and contacted the dean of the Notre Dame Law School when I applied. I tried in every way to pay the congressman back. When he asked, I had readily agreed to represent immigrant children and help families crossing the border in McAllen.

"Gabriela, this is Luis Moreno. Are you free to speak with me?"

"Certainly, Congressman Moreno. I always have time for you. How are you, sir?"

"I'm fine, Gabriela. I am calling because I want you to consider something seriously."

"What's that, sir?"

"I plan to retire and not run next November again. I want you to consider coming home and letting me announce my planned retirement and my desire to have you be our next congresswoman."

He spent the next fifteen minutes striking down each argument I made about why he should stay in office. I thought I had missed the filing deadline. I mentioned I didn't live in the district. I told him I could never fill his shoes. I said I was a lawyer and not a politician. I brought up the *National Tabloid* article with my near-naked photo on the front page. Since politics is a dirty business, I was certain any opponent would bring the article and photos to the voters' attention. I was worried that it would embarrass and hurt my mother.

The congressman had an answer for each of my protests, except my point that the *National Tabloid* journal article and photos would surface again and hurt my mother.

I told the congressman again that I was honored but that he was a legend and still loved by his constituents.

He told me that in politics, legends fade away quickly. "You are the legend around here after winning the case for the local high school teenager who the border patrol agents wrongfully detained near the border," he said. "The public will quickly rally around you."

Border patrol agents had stopped the teenage girl. They asked where she had been born. When she answered "Matamoras," they took her into custody and threatened to rape her if she didn't admit she was illegal. At first, the agency claimed that never happened. Later, they agreed to pay more than $250,000 to settle the case. Afterward, the story made the cover of a major news magazine and the front page of newspapers throughout the country. That led to Parker & McEvoy making an offer for me to leave home and come to Dallas. Now, that same case might be the impetus for me to go back home.

There was no way he or anyone else could keep the *National Tabloid* article from resurfacing, and nothing he could say would convince my mother. Could I do this and embarrass my mother again? I didn't know.

"You've taken me by surprise," I said. "I'm not sure I have finished what I set out to accomplish in Dallas. May I talk this over with my family and get back to you?"

"Certainly. Just keep in mind that the Rio Grande Valley needs a strong moderate advocate like you in Washington, and your family needs you back here with them."

"Yes sir. I'm interested in helping our community, and my family is important to me, but I never expected to come back and run for your seat in Congress."

My head was spinning. In all my career dreams, serving in Congress had not been one of them. I speed-dialed my father.

"Papá, I want to visit home and get your advice."

"Please don't tell me they asked you to represent another rich Dallas businessman."

"No, Papá. Luis Moreno is retiring and wants me to run for his seat and represent the Rio Grande Valley in Congress. I don't want to let the congressman down, but I have never thought about running for Congress and I need your thoughts."

He paused for a moment, and I knew what he was thinking. When he finally spoke, I discovered I had been right. "Have you thought about what photos of your near-naked body resurfacing would do to your mother?"

Then he said something I had never considered. "To be elected, you must spend hours courting your constituents, and you must raise a lot of money. That takes a lot of handshakes, kissing up to people you don't like, and pancake breakfasts. If you run, you must be sure that is how you want to spend your time when you are back home."

He was right. But I had other things to consider first. If I moved back home and ran for Congress, I would have to give up my relationship with Daniel. There was no way he was moving to Washington. I would have to give up my loyal assistant and friend, Lucia. There was no way she was moving to Washington. I would have to leave my law firm and give up my legal career. Those all weighed on my mind.

I say didn't anything about Hope to Congressman Moreno and I didn't factor her defense in my thinking about whether to run for Congress—until I saw a call from Father Michael. If I didn't defend Hope, there would be no problem. If I did defend her, I was not sure at that point whether I could still run for Congress.

The priest said something I had heard my father say many times. "Gabriela, the poor, especially the poor, need the very best lawyers helping them when they get in trouble. You are one of the best and Hope needs you."

He was right and my father had been right. He had spent a career helping the poor.

Chapter 6

Roberto

Lucia called Roberto Sanchez and told him she had booked a flight for him to fly to Baton Rouge through Dallas for the next day so he would be on the same flight as Gabriela.

Roberto was not happy. His daughter had assumed he was available and didn't have to be in court so he could meet her. He just shook his head.

"What's in Baton Rouge? Roberto asked.

"Gabriela will tell you."

"That's fine," Roberto said. But what can you tell me?"

Lucia replied, "A Dallas priest asked Gabriela to defend a teenage girl who is wanted for a murder in Dallas and has been arrested in Baton Rouge."

"I am surprised her law firm will allow her to defend an indigent teenage girl facing a murder charge."

"She hasn't told the firm because she plans to bow out of the case after she meets the girl in Baton Rouge."

Given her plan to bow out right away, Roberto wondered why his daughter wanted him to join her for her first meeting with her teenage client.

That afternoon, Roberto met Gabriela at the DFW gate where they would board their flight for Baton Rouge.

"Who is the teenage girl we are meeting in the Baton Rouge Jail?" Roberto asked after they boarded their flight.

"A seventeen-year-old girl named Hope Riley. She is wanted for murder in Dallas."

"You are a good person to take on her defense. Her future life will be in your hands. That is the most pressure you will ever face as a lawyer."

"Papá, I don't want to take on her defense. Even if I can deal with the stress, I don't have any experience representing a juvenile who is accused of murder, and my law firm will not get paid."

"Then I am not sure why we are here."

"We are here because I promised Father Michael I would help until Hope is returned to Dallas."

Gabriela told her father that the girls fled for Miami after shooting and killing a Dallas investment banker who apparently got off on having sex with underage teenagers, or at least the two girls who shot him.

Roberto frowned.

"You should defend her," he said. "If you don't help her, an overburdened public defender will be her lawyer."

"Papá, the public defender will have experience representing juveniles in felony cases. The public defender will know the prosecutor and most likely be able to work out a plea deal. I don't have the right experience."

Roberto had anticipated his daughter's reaction and he understood her reticence to defend the teenage girl. She had never defended a juvenile, a murder case, or a case in the Dallas County Court.

Roberto thought his daughter had also learned from watching what happened when he represented indigent clients. In his experience, those always became the most difficult cases. That was one reason she had left him for the big firm in Dallas.

But Roberto also knew his daughter's compassion for the underdog. He thought once Gabriela met the teenage girl, she would likely change her mind. He saved his questions about the case.

They ate dinner at a restaurant near their motel. Knowing his daughter's reluctance, he asked, "Can we continue discussing the teenager's case?"

"I am surprised you sought my permission. I know you want to continue, so go ahead."

"I can't believe the district attorney will want to prosecute the teenage girl. She was a victim. Henry Esposito was sexually abusing her."

"Okay. Just for the sake of our discussion, just suppose the district attorney doesn't see Hope as a victim, then there will be a trial. Suppose I decide to run for Congress, and I have this trial to handle before I can start campaigning."

"That won't happen," Roberto argued. "She's a juvenile. Cases in juvenile court move to completion quickly."

"Papá, Hope was seventeen the day Henry Esposito was shot. Texas is one of the few states that treats seventeen-year-old defendants as adults."

"Even so, any trial will be completed by March, giving you all the time you need to run for Congressman Moreno's seat. How bad can it get helping the girl?"

Gabriela put her palms on her face and shook her head.

"Winning the case will be difficult. A man was shot. That's a felony. Hope was there. In Texas, it makes no difference that she did not pull the trigger. Her future will depend on a jury finding her not guilty. That is a very heavy burden to put on any lawyer."

"At least hold your decision until you meet her."

"For you Papá, I will."

***

As soon as lawyer visitors were allowed the next morning, they entered the Baton Rouge Jail. After security screening, they were taken to an attorney's meeting room and waited to meet Hope Riley.

A guard escorted Hope into the meeting room. Roberto looked at the sultry-looking teenager with brown, wavy hair with golden blond streaks, parted down the middle hanging down below her shoulders, big brown eyes, and light bronze skin. He thought she had obviously used some of the money Esposito had given her to go to a high-end Dallas salon.

Roberto understood why Henry Esposito would be interested. She looked like a young model or actress with brown puppy-dog eyes. Her eyes sparkled even now as she was wiping away tears.

She was unusually tan for this time of year, and Roberto noticed a white spot on her wrist where she had apparently been wearing a watch. She had either been out in the sun somewhere or had been in a tanning bed wearing her watch.

When the guard left the three of them alone, Gabriela stood, and Hope fell into her arms and hugged her. When she pulled back, Roberto saw her trembling lips and slumped shoulders. Her body was shaking.

Gabriela told Hope that she remembered her from church, but he could tell Gabriela wasn't sure how to respond to the teenager other than staying calm and hoping that could make Hope feel calmer.

"Hope, my name is Gabriela Sanchez, and this is my father, Roberto Sanchez. We are your lawyers, and we are here to help you."

Hope was looking at Roberto as Gabriela continued.

"Okay. The first thing you should know is that anything you tell us is between us. We will never share anything you tell us with anyone, including your mother."

"Yes ma'am."

"It's okay for you to call me Gabriela. You don't need to say ma'am or Ms. Sanchez, okay?"

"Yes."

"Second, no one here in Baton Rouge and no one when you get to Dallas County Jail is your friend. No matter how nice anyone treats you, do not say anything about why you are in jail or what happened. You must keep everything to yourself, including talking with Amber if you see her."

Roberto looked her in the eye, waiting for a response. She seemed to still be in shock over her situation. Hope finally sighed, bowing her head.

"I've already talked to a police officer here."

"You did?" Gabriela asked. "What did you tell him?"

"I told him we shot Mr. Esposito and we were on our way to Miami. It is all on video."

Gabriela closed her eyes and shook her head. Roberto kept his eyes on Hope.

Roberto said, "Hope, we want to know more. It is important that you tell us the truth. Do you understand?"

Hope nodded.

"We need to know all about your social media posts, especially any that mention Henry Esposito," Gabriela said. "What electronic devices do you use?"

"I have an iPhone 12, an Apple Watch, and an iPad. I use Snapchat and Instagram primarily, but I also had a Facebook page. Mr. Esposito suggested that I post some of the photos he had taken on Snapchat and Instagram, and I did."

Gabriela handed Hope a sheet of paper and had her write down her login username and password for each site she used.

"Have you posted anything on any social media site about shooting Henry Esposito?"

"No."

"About going to Miami?"

"No."

"Can you tell us what happened the day Mr. Esposito was shot?"

"There's a lot I don't remember. I didn't feel well that day. I know that Amber and I took Uber to Henry Esposito's apartment and that when we arrived, he was cleaning a gun from his collection. He served birthday cake.

"Did Henry Esposito take photos of you and Amber that day?"

Hope rolled her eyes upward. "Yes. But he didn't take many of us together. He seemed to be more interested in taking photos and videos of Amber."

"Was that odd?" Gabriela asked.

"Yes. I don't remember another time when Mr. Esposito took photos of only one of us when we were at his apartment together."

"What happened after you ate the birthday cake?"

"I don't remember anything until I heard the loud pop from the gun. I ran into the room and saw Amber pull the trigger two more times and drop the gun. I looked at her and she had blood all over her. She was crying and looked stunned, as if she didn't know what she had done."

"You don't remember what happened until you heard the first shot? Why did you tell the police you and Amber shot and killed Henry Esposito?"

"Because when I couldn't remember, Amber told me I was there and nodded, which she thought meant she should pull the trigger."

Roberto had heard of people losing memory of traumatic events. That was important. But she had essentially confessed to the shooting and killing of Henry Esposito.

"You told the police you were with Amber when she fired the first shot, but now you say you don't remember anything before the first shot?" Roberto asked.

"I don't know. I remember feeling dizzy. I don't know why."

Hope started shaking, and Roberto feared she was having a panic attack. He could tell his daughter had never dealt with anyone having a panic attack. He calmly put his hand on Hope's wrist and told her to take slow, deep breaths.

It took a minute, but finally Hope calmed down.

Gabriela asked, "Did Amber tell you why she shot Henry Esposito?"

"No, I asked several times and she never told me," Hope replied.

Roberto made a note: *Accident defense!!!!*

"How did you meet Henry Esposito?" Gabriela asked.

"He was a judge at our school talent show and he saw me perform. Afterward, he met with me and told me my performance was remarkable and I had potential to be a star. He told me he would help me."

Roberto let Gabriela continue with the questions while he tried to determine if Hope was honestly answering what Gabriela asked.

"Why were you attracted to a man in his late thirties or forties?"

Roberto could almost recite her answer before she gave it. Esposito undoubtedly knew Hope did not have a father and probably knew her mother was working long hours to have money to raise her.

"He listened to me. I never had a father, so it was the first time an older man had listened to me. He believed in me and enabled me to believe in myself. He met me after school weekly for months, encouraging me and helping me. He told me he had connections and money and with that he could provide whatever I wanted. He showed me videos and told me he would help me become the next Britney Spears."

Roberto wrote another note: *A listening ear and* the *flattery trick...*

"Videos of Brittney Spears dancing and singing?" Gabriela asked.

"Yes. He told me she made her first appearance in the All-New Mickey Mouse Club when she was eleven, and by sixteen was one of the most famous people in the world."

"Why did you let him have sex with you the first time?"

Roberto was certain that Esposito had groomed her to the point that he knew she would let him have sex with her. Older men in the Rio Grande Valley had groomed teenage girls, and some of those girls had run away from home with the men.

"I don't even remember the first time. I believe it was several months after the talent show and our weekly meetings, but like I said, I don't remember for sure."

Roberto made a note and put a star by it, to remember what Hope had said. Gabriela looked over at his pad and saw the words: *Memory loss. Why did she confess to save her friend?*

"Why did you continue to let him have sex with you?" Gabriela asked.

Her head fell. When she lifted her head, tears streamed down her face. She looked at Roberto and then back at Gabriela.

"For my mother," Hope replied.

"Your mother?" Gabriela asked.

"My mother has sacrificed everything for me to be able to get acting and voice lessons. Mr. Esposito promised he would help me become a star. He hired an agent for me, a photographer to take photos for a portfolio. Because of Mr. Esposito, I had a small role in a movie made in Dallas. I made more money in a week than my mother made in a month. I dreamed about my future in Hollywood. When I made it, I planned to take the money I earned and build a house for my mother."

She bowed her head again.

"Did you ever tell your mother what you were doing and why you were having sex with Henry Esposito?" Gabriela asked.

"No, Mr. Esposito told me what we were doing should be kept a secret and that's what I did."

Before Gabriela could ask the next question, a guard entered the room and told Hope two Dallas policemen were there to take Hope and Amber back to Dallas.

"How can that be? Texas has not sought extradition." Roberto asked.

"She and her friend waived extradition this morning," the guard replied.

They tricked her, or her mother convinced her. "May we have one more minute?"

The guard left the room and Gabriela continued.

"Hope, why did you and Amber take Esposito's BMW and try to get away?"

Hope started to cry again. "I don't know. I don't know. I asked Amber why and she said if we told the police what happened no one would believe us. She said no one would look for us in Miami."

"Is there anything else you can tell me about what happened that day?"

Roberto saw Hope bite her bottom lip and tilt her head as if picturing the events of that day.

"No."

Roberto saw a gentle smile on his daughter's face. He knew she felt compassion for Hope. She would defend her now.

"Hope, before the day he was shot, the police came to your house and asked if Mr. Esposito was having sex with you. Your mother told me you said he wasn't. Why did you not tell the truth?" Gabriela asked.

Hope looked down and then at Gabriela, which Roberto took as a sign that her response would be truthful.

"I would never do anything to hurt Mr. Esposito. He was the kindest man I had ever met."

Roberto thought Esposito was having sex with several underage girls. So he must have spread his kindness around.

"Did you or Amber say anything to the Baton Rouge police when they arrested you?"

"Amber told the police we shot Esposito in self-defense. Later, she told them she didn't know the gun was loaded. They also took her to another room, and I don't know what she told them when she was alone."

"Were either of those stories true?" Gabriela asked.

"I don't know what happened. But we had agreed to tell the police she shot him in self-defense because we thought the police would let us go. That wasn't true, but I don't know if Amber thought the gun wasn't loaded or not."

The guard was back at the door.

When he left, Gabriela said, "Hope, one more thing before they take you away. Do not say anything in the police car, even to

Amber. Anything you say they can use against you. This is important. Do you understand?"

"Yes, but why can't I speak to Amber?"

"Because the police will hear anything you say, and because your friend Amber may turn against you," Gabriela responded.

"No way she would hurt me."

She already has, Roberto thought.

The guard re-entered and escorted a clearly shaken seventeen-year-old girl out the door in handcuffs.

When they were alone, Gabriela said, "She's confessed to the crime she didn't commit. If I defend her, I don't know how I can undo that."

Gabriela looked at her father and shook her head.

"You must find a way. You can't let them destroy this girl's life. Hope's not a murderer," Roberto said. "She had no motive to want Esposito dead. Even though she acts like an adult and liked the attention, Hope's a teenage victim of a predator, who manipulated her and started molesting her before she was old enough to drive."

I understood how Esposito manipulated her. When I was teenager, I thought I was in love with the San Antonio golf pro who my father had hired to teach me. I was vulnerable even though I had a wonderful family life. The golf pro had convinced me that he could make me a pro on the LPGA tour. It's that easy for a naïve teenage girl to be roped in. Esposito made Hope feel special.

"Papá, Hope acts like the innocent teenager. But I believe she was far less innocent even when she was only fifteen years old."

"What would you expect? I am sure even at fifteen she saw Esposito as the man who could help her make a career. So, you will defend her?" Roberto asked.

He heard a sigh coming from his daughter.

"My heart tells me I must defend Hope. My brain tells me defending her could ruin my chance to come home and become a congresswoman."

"Gabriela can do both. Do your best to get the district attorney to drop the charges."

"I will as soon as I meet with the prosecutor."

"Even being treated as an adult, I believe the case will be tried in March or at worst April," Roberto said.

"What if the trial is delayed?" Gabriela asked.

Roberto shot back, "What could possibly happen between now and March that would delay Hope's trial?"

Chapter 7

Gabriela

My father had encouraged me to defend Hope.

When I returned to Dallas that afternoon, I went directly to Jack Wainwright's office. His secretary wasn't at her station, but his door was open, so I knocked and entered after he motioned me to come in. Wainwright, the Parker & McEvoy managing partner, had always been uncomfortable around me since my first week with the law firm when he thought I was a secretary, not a lawyer.

"Gabriela, what brings you to see me?"

"Jack, I've decided to take on a case I thought you and the management committee should know about."

"Okay, what's the case?"

"Do you remember reading about Henry Esposito being murdered by two teenage girls?"

"Sure."

"I've been asked, and I've agreed to represent Hope Riley."

Wainwright shook his head. "Gabriela, we don't defend murder cases, especially those where the client cannot pay us. You can't take on this case without permission from the management committee, and I can tell you they won't give you permission."

Our firm was still a good old boys club, and a small group of older men made the rules for everyone but themselves. Getting permission to take on a case was only necessary because I had never been part of the inner circle. During my first year with the firm, a female partner had told me how I would be judged differently. "The partners in this firm will judge you solely by your accomplishments," she had said. "They will judge your young male colleagues by their potential."

"Father Michael asked me to represent Hope, and I know her mother."

"But the girl is not even Hispanic. She's a White girl. Unless the Catholic Diocese of Dallas is paying the firm, I don't care who asked you, or who you know," Wainwright said, raising his voice. "Our firm has a procedure that must be followed when a lawyer wants to take on a pro bono matter, and you didn't follow it. At best she's a prostitute."

"What difference does it make that she's White?"

"It means she doesn't need you defending her. Find a criminal defense lawyer, call the girl's mother and tell her your firm won't let you defend her daughter."

"Jack, I can't do that. Hope Riley is a victim of a child predator. If she is assigned a public defender, I'm not convinced she will receive the defense she deserves."

"You are the most gullible lawyer in our firm."

"What is that supposed to mean?"

"You believe everything the clients who can't pay us tell you. You believe the mothers and children who illegally cross our border claiming asylum. You believe this seventeen-year-old White girl who, as Henry Esposito lay dying, stole his car, and started driving to Miami. But when you defended Sparks Duval, the richest man in Texas, you didn't believe his story."

That hit a sore spot with me. Sparks Duval had hired a public relations firm and they had dictated how I would defend Duval, including convincing Duval to testify over my strenuous objection.

"Jack, it was the jury who didn't believe his story. I pleaded with him not to testify, and he did anyway. Even with that, I successfully defended Sparks Duval."

"You were only successful because of prosecutorial misconduct. The jury convicted Sparks."

"Isn't that what successful trial lawyers do?" I replied. "I found a way to win after the jury didn't believe our client. When can I meet with the management committee?"

"I will set up a meeting for tomorrow morning," Wainwright said.

"And what if they don't give me permission?"

"You'll either need to withdraw or leave the firm."

The next morning, I stood before the Parker & McEvoy management committee in the John Royster room on the thirty-seventh floor. I surveyed the room of four men in their fifties and one woman in her forties. I looked at the screen on the wall where Robert Mason and Jane Swanson had joined the meeting from Austin. If body language was any indication, the committee had already decided.

Jack Wainwright stood before the group and faced the camera at the far end of the conference room.

"Our partner, Gabriela Sanchez, has asked to meet with us after she agreed to take on a pro bono case defending a seventeen-year-old girl accused of murdering the Dallas financier, Henry Esposito. Gabriela has acknowledged that she did not seek the management committee's permission prior to agreeing to represent the girl. Gabriela is aware that our firm does not defend murderers, and she herself has no experience defending a murder case. She has asked permission to speak with you and ask your permission to take the case. With that, I will turn it over to Gabriela."

"Thank you, Jack.

"Jack asked me why we should take on a murder case defending a young girl who can't pay us. I suppose the simple answer is because it is the right thing to do. Hope Riley, the girl I plan to defend, is seventeen years old. Hope's not a murderer. She's a high school student. Henry Esposito, a rich man in his forties, victimized Hope. He groomed her by leading her to believe he could build her modeling, acting, singing career.

"Hope didn't pull the trigger. She didn't even know the gun was loaded when her friend pulled the trigger."

Jack Wainwright interrupted. "You've never defended a juvenile. You've never defended a murder case."

"Jack," I began. "Hope Riley had the misfortune of having her seventeenth birthday on the ninth of November, the day her friend shot Henry Esposito. Seventeen-year-old girls and boys are tried as adults in Texas, one of only a handful of states that automatically put seventeen-year-old boys and girls in the adult system. Had the girls shot Esposito the day before her birthday, she would be treated as a juvenile."

"Well, then, you've never defended a criminal case in Dallas County Criminal Court," Wainwright responded.

"Jack, you weren't worried when I defended my first federal criminal case in the Northern District Court."

"Have you considered the possibility that your client seduced Henry Esposito for his money?"

"Jack, Hope was fifteen when Henry Esposito first had sex with her. He judged a talent show. He visited her afterward. She didn't know him before that day."

Wainwright shook his head. "How do you respond to not seeking permission before you agreed to defend your client?" he asked.

"Jack, I am a partner in this firm. The lawyers sitting around this table and watching on TV monitors, and many of our other partners who are not here or watching have taken on many client matters, including pro-bono without asking the management committee's permission. Do you want me to start reciting a list of those clients?"

Wainwright shook his head with a smirk on his face, but I continued.

"Emma Riley worked two jobs as many as sixteen hours a day so her daughter Hope could have a better life. I took this case so her sacrifice will not be for nothing and to save her daughter from being denied the opportunity to finish high school, go to college, get a job that she loves, and lead a productive life. I read something recently that applies to Hope Riley. She is not able to vote, serve on a jury, or serve in the military, and Texas wants to not help her as a victim, but instead, ruin the rest of her life by trying her as an adult. I can't and won't let this happen to her."

"Very noble," Jack Wainwright said. "But noble causes don't pay our rent. The girl is a prostitute who was willing to have sex with a man old enough to be her father to make money. This case is going to bring to light a major scandal in Dallas, and it may touch some of our most important clients. Once you start down the path of representing a client in a criminal case, it could consume you and no judge will let you withdraw, unless one of our clients is implicated."

"I know all of that, Jack."

Chuck Green stood at the far end of the table. He was one of the good old boys, so I expected him to be lock step with Jack Wainwright.

"Jack," Green said and then asked, "What do you want us to do—expel Gabriela from the firm? Dock her pay?"

Wainwright stood. "Chuck, the firm must have some rules on the kind of client matters we are willing to take. Representing a teenage girl accused of murder does not fit the profile of clients we want to represent."

Chuck Green looked over at me. "Who asked you to defend this girl?"

"A priest from my parish called me. When I told him I had not represented a minor or a person accused of murder, he asked if I would meet with Hope's mother. He said Emma Riley knew me from church. I agreed to meet with her. They both pleaded with me to help Hope. At first, I didn't want to defend her, and I told them so."

"And what made you change your mind?"

"I met her. I could see right away the hurt in her eyes, and I knew that she was a victim, even though she didn't think she was. We all know that teenage girls are trafficking victims throughout Texas. I saw it first-hand. Back when I was in high school, a so-called pimp kidnapped one of my friends. She spent months away from home taking drugs and being sold to men. When she came home, she was never the same. She could never get off drugs.

"What can you tell us about her codefendant?"

"Her name is Amber Davis, and she was one of Hope's friends from school. Amber is sixteen, so I expect the district attorney to deal with her in juvenile court and not be a codefendant. Amber shot Esposito three times and killed him. Hope heard the first shot and tried to stop her friend. I believe Amber is the leader and Hope the follower. Amber lives in a foster home because her mother is in prison for drugs and her father abandoned the family. I don't know much more about her at this point."

Chuck Green paused for a moment. He had taught me that pausing was one way to elevate the importance of what he would say next. "I, for one, believe Gabriela should defend Hope. I recently read that at any one time, seventy-nine thousand minors are being trafficked in Texas. The governor vetoed a bill that would have decriminalized prostitution for children. I believe our firm gains positive recognition by representing a young seventeen-year-old girl who became the victim of a rich man. There are times when we must do what will best serve our community. This is one of those times. I urge you all to support Gabriela."

Green's unflinching support surprised me. Wainwright scowled, which I took to mean Green surprised him as well.

"What if she is guilty or the jury finds her guilty. How will the firm benefit from that?" Wainwright asked.

"Even if Hope is guilty or found guilty the girl is a victim of abuse. We will have done the right thing for the right reasons. Jack, sometimes we should go back to when law was a profession not just a business."

Wainwright shook his head.

"Does anyone else care to speak?" Jack Wainwright asked.

"Hearing no one wishing to speak, we should take a vote."

Chuck Green stood. "Jack, what exactly are we voting on?"

Wainwright responded. "Whether to allow Gabriela Sanchez to defend Hope Riley or demand she withdraw before any court hearing."

I left the room while the management committee voted. Although I preferred not to, I was prepared to leave the firm if that became necessary to represent Hope. I knew if Jack Wainwright came out of the meeting, that would mean the management committee voted against me, but if Chuck Green came out to deliver the news, that would mean the committee voted in my favor.

Fifteen minutes later, the door to the conference room slowly opened. I got up to see Chuck Green walking toward me.

He smiled. "You won the firm's blessing to defend Hope. But I urge you to do whatever it takes to get the case settled or win her acquittal quickly. Each month while the case is pending, you'll hear about it from Jack."

"Thank you for supporting me Chuck," I replied.

Green smiled and walked away.

My stomach was in knots. I had won the fight to defend Hope; now I had to face the war to persuade a jury to find her not guilty.

Chapter 8

Hope

When the police car arrived in Dallas, they dropped Amber off at a building that Hope thought looked like a school. When she started to get out of the car, one of the policemen told her they were taking her to a different jail, the one that housed adults, not juveniles. That made no sense to Hope since she and Amber were both teenagers.

A few minutes later they arrived at a building that was several stories high. It looked more like a jail than where they had dropped off Amber. A policeman escorted Hope in handcuffs through a door, where a woman in a police uniform took over.

The uniformed officer walked with Hope to a room with a sign that read "Intake." The officer opened a thick metal door and walked with Hope over to a room where she told Hope to take off all her clothes. The officer then visually inspected Hope, including having Hope open wide each of her body cavities. Hope felt afraid, humiliated, and embarrassed, but there was nothing she could do about it.

After the strip search, the officer handed Hope a red striped jail jumper, two pairs of underwear, and a pair of the ugliest shoes she had ever seen. Then she was taken to another room where her photo was taken and a man in uniform took her fingerprints.

Another officer escorted Hope to another tower, where she was taken to a floor specifically for teenagers. Hope was placed in a cell by herself. She felt claustrophobic, alone, and bored in her small six feet by twelve feet cell.

While she was alone, Hope could still hear boys on her floor. When she asked why the boys weren't alone and she was, a guard told Hope that she was alone because there were no other teenage girls in the jail at that time.

At first, Hope thought being alone would be okay. But as hours dragged on and she had no phone, no computer, not even a book to keep her occupied, she became more anxious. At 4:30 p.m., a guard slipped a tray with her dinner into her cell. Hope could barely look at what was on the tray, much less eat it.

With nothing else to do, Hope decided to go to sleep early. That was when she discovered her only choice was a bench with a mat and no pillow. It was extremely uncomfortable, and it took at least an hour before she fell asleep. During the night, Hope woke up several times, never knowing the time or whether she should get up.

Finally, a guard placed a tray with breakfast in her cell. This time, Hope decided to eat. Later that morning, when Hope asked the guard if there was a book she could read, the guard handed Hope a Bible. Looking for something to keep her occupied, Hope began reading.

A few hours later, a guard brought her a tray with lunch. It was a bologna sandwich. It looked as terrible as it tasted.

After dinner, a guard told Hope she had visitors and escorted Hope to a room where she found her mother and Father Michael. Hope went to hug her mother and was told no touching was allowed.

"Mama, you have to get me out of here. I can't stand it."

"We hope we can raise money for your bail," Father Michael said.

"What if you can't raise the money?" Hope asked. "This place is awful. I don't even have a pillow to sleep on. I don't know what time it is, what day it is, and the only book I can read is the Bible."

"That is not a bad book to be reading," Father Michael said, smiling. "There are many stories in the Bible that will inspire you to hang in while you are here."

Hope started crying. "You can't imagine what it's like in here. Right now, I am the only girl on the floor. I have no one I can talk to. I was told I would have one hour out of my tiny cell to exercise. When I go to the bathroom or take a shower, someone is watching me. It's awful."

"Gabriela Sanchez will help you get out," Emma Riley said. "You can count on her to save you."

Through her tears, Hope said, "Mama, I am so sorry to let you down, but I shouldn't be here in the first place. I did nothing wrong. I didn't shoot the gun. I didn't even know the gun was loaded."

Hope saw her mother look over at Father Michael, who shook his head. Hope knew her mother had wanted to tell her that she and Amber should not have taken Esposito's money, his gun, and fled to Florida in his BMW.

After a few minutes, their visit was over, and a guard escorted Hope back to her cell. As she lay down on the bench, Hope thought about what her mother had said about Ms. Sanchez. Was she Hope's only hope? She had already forgotten how getting arrested had ruined her future. All she could think about was that she had to get out of jail one way or another.

That night, all Hope could think about was her life before Henry Esposito judged the talent show. She felt like she had come so far from when she had been in special education in grade school and her classmates had made fun of her. That embarrassment was something she had never forgotten, but it had been the source of her motivation.

Her mom had loved her very much, but she didn't totally understand her challenges. Her mom would give her a list of things to do, and Hope would fail because without writing each task down, she would forget. She had learned to compensate and if she could see what was on the list, she could easily remember each task. That ability to see and remember had served her well when she began acting. She could sing, dance, and learned how to act. When she was in the spotlight, no one had made fun of her.

She had lived alone with her mother, who inspired Hope to pursue her education and go to college. She had been doing well in school, had a boyfriend who adored her, and had been a star on her high school track team. Hope had followed all the rules: no smoking, no alcohol, no sex, and as a result, no fun. On the one hand, she had high hopes for her future: go to college on a scholarship. On the other hand, Hope didn't care about college. She had wanted to model and had wanted a photographer to create a photo portfolio book for her. That was what Henry Esposito had promised and had done and sent to modeling agencies.

Her mother, Father Michael, and her lawyer all thought that Henry Esposito had exploited her. Nothing could have been further from the truth. If anything, she had exploited him. She learned that older men were interested in her when a teacher had groped her when she was a freshman in high school. Instead of being offended, she played along and let him touch her. Hope liked the attention. After the talent show, she had dumped her boyfriend and had willingly started the sexual relationship with Henry Esposito. The first time he had sex with her had been the best day of her life. Since she never knew her father, Esposito had been the first man who had made Hope feel safe and loved.

Hope desperately wanted to be found not guilty, but she didn't want Ms. Sanchez to claim Mr. Esposito was a bad man for having sex with her, even if it hurt her case. It simply wasn't true. She had been the aggressor, not him. He had made her feel like an adult, and she liked that feeling.

CHAPTER 9

Junior Jones

Junior Jones was the public defender who worked in the Dallas Juvenile Court. He had been appointed to represent Amber Davis; the sixteen-year-old girl accused of murdering a Dallas investment banker. This was his first murder case, and he knew the prosecutors were out for blood.

Junior's first goal was to persuade the juvenile-court judge to not certify Amber to be tried as an adult. Looking at her file before he met her, Junior wondered why Amber had shot the man who was paying her five-hundred dollars or more each time she visited him, and one thousand dollars when she did threesomes with Hope. He planned to argue that Amber was the victim of sex trafficking by the victim, Henry Esposito.

When Junior first met Amber, she at first wouldn't even talk to him. He explained to her that he was her lawyer and he was there to help her. She still wouldn't respond.

After introducing himself and telling Amber he was the public defender appointed to represent her, Junior said, "Amber, the district attorney lawyer handling your case has told me that they plan to charge you with murder and ask that you be certified by the juvenile judge to be tried as an adult. They may try to send you to prison for the rest of your life. Do you understand how serious that is?"

Amber nodded.

"My job is to persuade the judge to treat you as a juvenile, not an adult. I can't do that without your help."

Amber nodded again but didn't say anything.

He looked at the report in his hands and reminded Amber that she had claimed when first questioned that she had shot Esposito in self-defense. Later, when the police were ready to give her a lie detector test, Amber had changed her story and said she didn't know the gun Esposito had given her was loaded.

Junior said, "Amber, tell me what really happened."

He saw her mouth fall open and he heard her gasp, but she didn't say what happened.

Junior continued telling Amber that the first step in the process was to go before a juvenile judge in a hearing to determine whether she should be detained. Amber tilted her head and touched it, which Junior took to mean she was confused. He explained that in the hearing, the judge would determine whether there was sufficient evidence to keep her in the juvenile justice center. Amber seemed to grasp what that meant. Junior told Amber that because of the seriousness of her crime, and her ever-changing story, the judge would rule that she should continue to be detained.

Junior explained that after the detention hearing, a judge would decide whether her case should remain in juvenile court or whether Amber should be certified to be tried as an adult. He told her that in that process, both she and her mother would be served with a petition. Junior also explained that in Texas, the prosecutor could seek determinative sentencing as an alternative to certification to be tried as an adult. If the prosecutor sought determinative sentencing, Amber would have the opportunity for rehabilitation.

Amber finally spoke and told Jones that her mother was in prison and that she had been in foster care the last two years. She showed him a paper that had been handed to her before she met with him.

At least Amber started talking, he thought. He told Amber that the law required that the authorities give her a full diagnostic study, including a social evaluation, investigation, and circumstances of the offense. Amber threw up her hands, palms up, suggesting she did not understand what he had just told her.

He explained that because she had shot and killed a man, that would weigh against her being tried as a juvenile, but he urged her to cooperate with the doctors or social workers because it would be important to stay in the juvenile court system and be given the opportunity to rehabilitate rather than be sent to prison.

"Do you understand what I have told you?" Junior asked.

"Yes, sir," Amber replied. "If my trial is in juvenile court, I may not be sent to prison, but if my trial is in the adult court, I will most likely be sent to prison."

"Good. Your case has been assigned to a prosecutor who prefers to keep first-time offenders in the juvenile system, especially victims of trafficking. When you are asked, explain how you met Henry Esposito and what he and his friends were doing to you."

"Yes, sir. What is trafficking?"

"Esposito and his friends paid you to have sex with them. You were a victim."

"No. I wasn't. I wanted the money. High school boys push me to have sex with them for free. I had sex with men for money before I met Esposito. I wanted to buy clothes and a cell phone. I wasn't a victim. I asked Hope if I could be part of what she was doing to earn money. When I visited my mother in prison, she told me I should earn as much money as possible because I could help her appeal her conviction or be paroled."

"Amber, under the law, anyone under eighteen who is paid in exchange for sex is a victim. So even if you did not feel like a victim, you were under the law. Never, never say to anyone that you weren't a victim. Do you understand?"

"Yes, sir."

"Did Mr. Esposito give you drugs the day you shot him?"

"No, he never gave me drugs, nor did any of the other men, even when I asked."

"You claimed at first you shot Esposito in self-defense. Then you changed your story. I need to know if your second story is true. Did you know his gun was loaded?"

Amber looked away from him at the far wall.

"What do you want me to say?"

Junior thought Amber was capable of lying at any time.

"I want you to tell me the truth," he said, raising his voice.

Amber fidgeted. "Isn't it best if I say I didn't know it was loaded?"

"You heard me," Junior responded, raising his voice. "Tell me the truth!"

"I didn't know whether it was loaded or not."

"Did Mr. Esposito select the gun he wanted you to hold?"

"Yes. He was cleaning a gun. Hope had picked it up and given it to me, but that was at least an hour before I shot Mr. Esposito. During the hour, Esposito took photos of the two of us with his gun."

"Did he or Hope tell you the gun was loaded?"

Amber stared at the wall again.

"No," she finally replied.

"Why did you pull the trigger?"

Amber gazed at the ceiling for just a moment.

"We were just playing. I don't know," she said. "The first time I pulled the trigger I heard a click, but no bullet was loaded.

"Why did you continue pulling the trigger?"

"It just happened. I can't tell you why."

"And the second time you pulled the trigger, you shot Esposito?"

"Yes. It all happened so fast," Amber replied. "Hope was screaming, and I panicked."

Junior wrote on his legal pad. *Hope was back in the room and witnessed the shooting.*

"Where did you shoot him?"

"I think the bullet pierced his shoulder."

"Why didn't you stop shooting after the first bullet hit him?"

"I don't know—everything happened so fast."

"Whose idea was it to take his BMW?"

"Mine. I thought no one would believe our story. I just wanted to get as far away as possible before anyone found his body. We never planned to keep the BMW. It was the only way we could get out of Dallas right then and there."

"Who were the other men Mr. Esposito arranged to have sex with you?"

"I'd rather not say."

"Why? I'm your lawyer—I need to know everything."

"I'm afraid of what might happen to me if I tell you."

"Why are you afraid?"

"Does it really matter? I'm afraid because these men have lots of money and they don't want their secrets to be told. One of the men is a policeman. He could easily have someone hurt me while I am in here. Another man is a lawyer. Another man is a contractor."

"Did the other men pay you to have sex with them?"

"Yes."

"So, when the other men had sex with you, Esposito paid you and the men also paid you?"

"Yes, those were the best days. I earned four hundred dollars."

"What did you do with the money you were paid?"

"I went shopping. I bought clothes and shoes, a cell phone, a computer, and a tablet. I gave two thousand dollars to my mother. But she needed more money to hire a lawyer. That was why I wanted Mr. Esposito to let me be there for his friends."

"Your mother wanted you to prostitute yourself?"

"My mother just wanted me to make money for her. She knew how I earned the money, and she didn't care. How else can someone my age earn four hundred dollars in an hour?"

Junior shook his head, not knowing what to make of a mother, even one in prison, encouraging her teenage daughter to be a prostitute.

"Okay. Take advantage of the classes they offer you while you are in here. If nothing else, it will help you pass the time more easily."

Amber smiled. "Yes sir. I'll do that."

With what he had learned about her so far, Junior took Amber's smile to mean that she would do whatever it took to con the staff that she was a model prisoner.

As he got up to leave, he said, "One more thing. No more stories. Don't talk to anyone about your case. You've already told two far different accounts of what happened."

"What if someone asks me what happened?"

"Say that your lawyer told you not to talk about it."

"Yes, sir."

A week later, Junior received a copy of Amber's diagnostic study. He knew most of what he read, including her mother having been in and out of prison for drug-related offenses and prostitution. Amber's father had abandoned the family after Amber's mother was arrested when Amber was six, and her brother, Ray, was four. They had been in foster care for several years. Amber had a criminal record that included the petty crime of shoplifting and stealing a car.

During the interview, Amber had lied to the evaluators when she told them that she had been sexually molested by a construction worker when she was twelve. According to court records. Amber had had several sexual encounters starting when she was thirteen. The evaluators had stated that she had even initiated sexual encounters with grown men.

Based on their interview with Amber, the evaluators did not believe she intended to kill Henry Esposito and they believed Amber and Hope had stolen Esposito's BMW and his cash because they were convinced no one would believe their story or what Esposito had been doing to them for close to two years. Hope Riley had recruited Amber when Amber was fourteen years old, and Esposito had exploited and taken advantage of a young fourteen-year-old girl who had no money and no other opportunity to earn it. Esposito had been the one to hand her a loaded pistol, and Amber didn't know it was loaded when she pulled the trigger. At the end of the report, the evaluators concluded that despite the seriousness of the offense and their concern about the toll taking a life has on society, Amber could still be remediated and become a normal law-abiding adult.

Junior had anticipated that conclusion, but he knew the prosecutor would demand Amber testify against Hope before she would go along with the recommendation.

Junior called Gabriela Sanchez to give her an update.

"I think I can work out a deal for Amber," Junior said.

"That's encouraging. What kind of deal?"

"The prosecutor filed charges and asked for a determinate sentence. We waived the right to a grand jury and the judge approved the determinate sentence."

Gabriela couldn't resist. "What is a determinate sentence?"

"I forgot you haven't dealt with any juvenile cases. A determinate sentence is an alternative to certifying a juvenile and trying her as an adult. The sentence remains in the juvenile system until the juvenile turns nineteen. At that point she can potentially be transferred to the adult prison, or if she does well, she could be paroled. My goal is for Amber to be released when she turns nineteen."

"So, what are you doing?"

"I have suggested that Amber plead to manslaughter and theft of Esposito's vehicle, and in return I am hoping her sentence will be in the juvenile system and I hope she will be released without going to the adult prison."

Junior expected that since Gabriela had never defended a juvenile, she most likely had never heard of determinate sentencing or a plea called "true."

"Can you explain what that plea means?" Gabriela asked.

"It's the juvenile plea of guilty. That is the term that is used."

"That would be a great deal for Amber."

"I agree," Junior replied. "But there's one thing you should know."

Junior heard a deep breath on the other end of the phone.

"What's that?" Gabriela asked.

"The district attorney will require Amber to identify the other men who paid her to have sex and testify against your client in her trial. So far, she refuses to identify the other men."

"Then why are you telling me?"

"Because the district attorney said he would agree to the manslaughter plea I have outlined also if Amber testifies against your client."

"What would Amber say?" Gabriela asked.

"Amber will testify that Hope told her she wanted Esposito to stop abusing her. Then she will say Hope was the one who handed her Esposito's gun and that Hope nodded when Amber was holding the gun, which was the signal to pull the trigger. They need her testimony to justify a murder charge against your client. I am sorry, but I wanted you to know."

"Damn," Gabriela replied. "Hope wasn't even in the room when Amber fired the first shot."

"You mean that is what she will say. Her jury will have to decide."

CHAPTER 10

Amber

Amber didn't like or respect her court-appointed lawyer. She had learned more about the juvenile criminal justice system when she talked to her mother. Amber understood that she must follow the rules and express remorse for shooting Henry Esposito. She could do that. It would be worth it in the end, she thought. The sooner she was out of jail the sooner she could get to Miami.

Amber didn't want to testify against Hope. She hoped to find a way to avoid it if possible. She loved Hope and hated that she might be the one to send her friend to jail. She never understood why Hope was more interested in boys and in Henry Esposito than her.

Why hadn't Hope spoken to her during the entire trip from Baton Rouge in the police car? With no speaking between them, Amber was unsure what story they would tell the police. Did she shoot Esposito in self-defense, or would they say she didn't know the gun was loaded?

Amber thought back to the day Hope showed her the two one-hundred-dollar bills in Hope's wallet. She had suspected that some man was paying Hope to have sex with him. Hope told her that day what had been going on with Henry Esposito and invited her to a party Esposito had planned for Saturday night. Hope told her she might earn as much as five hundred dollars.

College-aged guys had paid Amber for sex before, but not one had ever paid two hundred dollars. Hope was willing to get her into the action.

They had spent that day shopping for a black dress, thigh-high stockings, and heels. Henry Esposito had given Hope five hundred dollars for the purchases, and they had spent every penny. She looked hot that night, and several of Esposito's friends had spoken to her. A young man who said his name was Randy and who she thought was in his thirties finally won out. He had taken Amber to a nearby hotel and had given her five crisp one-hundred-dollar bills. Amber couldn't believe it. She kept three hundred dollars for herself and sent her mother the other two hundred, and she never told Hope how much she had been paid.

When she thought about it, Amber realized that the work she had done to earn the money had taken less than an hour. The rest of the time they'd talked. She had learned from her mother how to act interested in a man and to touch his neck or arm or shoulder and look into his eyes when he told his story.

Shortly after she arrived at the juvenile facility, Amber had started taking classes. She wasn't much interested in school or the classes, but she wanted to make everyone believe she was so they would tell the judge that she was a good candidate for rehabilitation.

None of the men who Henry Esposito had set up with her came to visit. That came as no surprise.

A well-dressed lawyer in a blue pin-striped suit came to visit her. He handed her a business card and she read his name: Vincent Rizzo.

"Amber, I am here to represent you."

"Why?" she asked.

"Because you have your whole life ahead of you and you do not want to spend any of it behind bars in a state prison."

"But why do you care about me? I have no money to pay you."

"I care about you because I believe you deserve the best lawyer, and I am that lawyer. I may even be able to get money to help you."

Amber knew Mr. Rizzo wasn't representing her, or offering her money, out of the goodness of his heart. One or more of the men with whom she had sex were paying Rizzo to make sure she didn't remember anything about them.

"Have the police asked you who paid you to have sex?" Rizzo asked.

"Yes."

"What did you tell them?"

"I didn't know who they were because they and I went by made-up names." That was a lie, but she thought Mr. Rizzo would be pleased. "My name was Monique. None of the men knew my first and last name, other than Henry Esposito."

"If you want to have a future, don't ever give any names—even made-up names. They may try to show you photos of Mr. Esposito's friends. You must not recognize any of the photos. Do you understand? Your former clients will make sure you have a great future, but you must not disclose anything about them."

"I understand, but my lawyer, Mr. Jones, told me the police and the prosecutor want me to identify the men who had sex with me as part a manslaughter plea deal so I can be out on parole when I turn nineteen."

"Don't plead true to manslaughter. I can get you a better deal, plus you will have some money when you are released. Hang tight and simply do not remember who the men were or what they looked like. I assume you didn't take photos of any of the men on your phone. Is that correct?"

"I wasn't allowed to have my phone when I was with them."

"Did any of the men offer to send money or deposit money for you in Miami?"

"No. I didn't have any contact with any of the men after I shot Mr. Esposito. We were going to Miami because it was Gucci?"

"Gucci?"

"Yeah, as you would say a really cool place."

"Good. If you cooperate with me, you will have money waiting for you when you complete your juvenile detention."

"How much money?"

"That depends on how well you cooperate. What else can I do for you?"

"Get my mother out of prison. I need her now."

"What is your mother's name?"

"Ramona Davis."

"If you follow my instructions, in addition to the money, I will do my best to get your mother released from prison and help the two of you move on with your life."

Amber knew that Rizzo was the lawyer for at least one of the men with whom she had had sex, but that didn't matter if Rizzo paid her a lot of money and could get her mother out of prison. She decided to get rid of Junior Jones and replace him with Mr. Rizzo.

A few days later, Mr. Rizzo came by again. When they were alone, he said, "I visited your mother. She will have a parole hearing in six months. I will represent her."

Amber smiled.

"That's not all," Rizzo continued. "I convinced the prosecutor to let you plead true to a criminally negligent homicide. You'll be in the juvenile system. If you behave, you will be released on parole when you turn nineteen."

"What do they expect from me?" Amber asked.

"You must plead true to criminally negligent homicide and testify against your friend Hope when she goes to trial. You must testify that she handed you the loaded gun and either told you or gave a sign to pull the trigger."

Junior Jones had told her the same condition. Amber was torn. Through thick and thin Hope had been her most loyal friend. She had been like a big sister, having numerous times given her advice and guidance. Hope had given her the opportunity to go to Henry Esposito's parties and make lots of money. She had even agreed to lie about the shooting to save Amber. Hope would never betray Amber, and now Amber was being asked to betray Hope to stay out of prison.

Rizzo must have noticed something because when Amber looked up, he said, "It's up to you. Will you be okay going to prison for the rest of your life, or do you want to go home when you're nineteen and be with your mother?"

Chapter 11

Gabriela

I had never visited a client in the Dallas County Jail, much less a seventeen-year-old client. After going through security, a sergeant responsible for the teenage floor escorted me to the sixth floor of the jail. I entered a room with a table and chairs and saw Hope sitting, waiting for me.

Hope looked far different from when I had met her in Baton Rouge. Her hair was a tangled mess. Her eyes were red and wet. Her neck was bent down, and she had a vacant stare. I wasn't sure where to begin. I had never represented a client who looked like they had already given up.

"Hope, I'm sorry. I know this must be extremely hard for you."

"Ms. Sanchez, you've got to get me out of here. I am bored out of my mind and I am going crazy in this place. I'm the only girl here. I sit in my cell with nothing to do most all of the day. I can't eat the food because it tastes awful. Can you help me get out of here?"

The judge had set Hope's bail at one million dollars. So unless someone came up with sufficient money, or the judge reduced the bond, I would not be able to get Hope released.

"Can you tell me what is going to happen to me?" Hope asked.

I had prepared a chart showing step by step. I placed it on the table for Hope to see.

"First, on Thursday, you will be arraigned. At your arraignment, the clerk will read the charges against you and ask how you plead."

"What will be the charges against me?"

"Amber is seeking a manslaughter charge rather than a murder charge. I hope they won't charge you with murder."

"How could they charge me with murder? I never touched the gun. I didn't know the gun was even loaded. The last thing I wanted was for Mr. Esposito to be dead. He had promised to help me become a model and an actress and I had already modeled and had a small role in a movie."

"I know," I replied. "I have told the district attorney all of those points. They will charge you with theft of Esposito's BMW."

"It wasn't my idea. Amber came up with the idea of fleeing to Miami in his BMW."

"True, but you went along with it. You drove the car."

Hope's eyes closed. She grimaced and slowly shook her head.

"During the hearing I will ask the judge to reduce the bail, but we will be fighting an uphill battle," I said.

Hope's eyes teared up.

"I've got to get out of here. I can't stand being here."

I thought about what to say. I had no experience consoling a seventeen-year-old girl stuck in a cell by herself for almost the entire day. I thought about what my mother would have said to me and I was still at a loss.

"I will do my best, Hope. You have to stay strong."

"I can't stay strong."

"Hope, did Henry Esposito ever set you up to have sex with his friends?"

"No. He asked me if I wanted to make more money by being with his friends and I said no. Mr. Esposito never made me do anything I didn't want to do. He made that promise the first time he took photos of me naked, and he never broke his promise. Everything I did for him I had given my permission."

***

Two days later, I stood with Hope before Judge Amy Foster, who asked the clerk to read the charges.

"Hope Jessica Riley, you are charged with murder, grand theft, human trafficking, and contributing to the exploitation of a minor, how do you plead?"

Hope replied, "Not guilty."

I was stunned. I understood the grand theft charges, but how could they charge Hope with murder and human trafficking?

When a guard led Hope away, I turned to Robin Polk. I didn't know her, but I had heard she was a hard ass and that defense lawyers had accused her of prosecutorial misconduct.

"Ms. Polk, Henry Esposito was a predator. I was hoping when you learned that Hope was a victim you would drop the charges against her."

"Ms. Sanchez, are you saying Esposito deserved to die? I may agree with you, but in Texas that is not a defense to murder."

"She didn't shoot him," I said.

"But she was there with her friend she had recruited, and they fled after shooting Esposito."

"How could you charge her with human trafficking and exploitation of a minor?" I asked. "Hope's a victim, not a trafficker, and she herself was a minor when you claim she exploited a minor."

Robin Polk turned and stared at me before answering. "She recruited Amber Davis for Henry Esposito and he paid Hope when she brought Amber to him. That's trafficking pure and simple."

I shook my head, trying to convey my disgust to Polk. "If anything, Amber begged Hope to let her participate because she wanted the money."

Polk approached me once again as if trying to intimidate me. "She'll testify that it was the other way around," she said. "You can make your points on cross-examination."

"Her lawyer told me Amber refuses to identify the other men who paid her for sex."

"That's true, but we are confident she will come around to avoid going from the juvenile system to prison when she comes of age."

Afterward, I found Hope in the holding cell. She was crying.

"What does human trafficking mean?

"They say that Henry Esposito paid you to recruit Amber to have sex with him and with you in front of him. Did he pay you?"

Hope looked away.

"Mr. Esposito gave me a Gucci handbag and paid me five hundred dollars the first time Amber came with me to a party he held. He paid us one thousand dollars every time we had a threesome with him. But I didn't recruit her. Amber had been meeting guys from a Backpage ad she created. Those guys paid her only one hundred dollars. When she discovered she could make more than double that from men less likely to beat her, she begged me to let her come with me."

"How did she even know you were seeing Mr. Esposito?"

"She found two one-hundred-dollar bills in my wallet and pressured me to tell her how I earned that money. When she went with me, Mr. Esposito told her that he had friends who would want to be with her."

"The attorney who will prosecute you says Amber will testify that you recruited her."

"She won't say that. Esposito regularly had parties with his friends and Amber asked me if she could go with me. If she says I recruited her, she'll be lying. And one more thing about Amber."

"What about her?"

"I believe she intended to kill Mr. Esposito."

I was stunned for a moment. That was about the last thing I expected Hope to tell me.

"What?"

"She intended to kill him."

"What makes you believe she intended to kill him?"

"It was the look she had in her eyes when I came in the room after the first shot. I screamed, she looked at me and shot him two more times."

"Why would she want to kill him? He was paying her and so were his friends."

"I don't know. The only thing I know is it wasn't because he and his friends were having sex with her. She liked the money he and his friends gave her even more."

Why did Amber shoot and kill Esposito? I needed a motive I could promote with the jury. But, even if Amber had a powerful motive, how did she know he would bring out a loaded pistol that day? *Hope can't answer that. Amber is the only one who knows.*

CHAPTER 12

Gabriela

The next morning, I opened the app to the Dallas newspaper and found Hope's color jail photo in her striped suit was on the front page. Below Hope's photo I read an article about her arraignment, denial of her bail reduction, and reporting that in addition to murder, the state had charged Hope with grand theft and trafficking a minor for sex.

I saw Hope's eyelids and the corners of her mouth drawn down. She looked defeated before we had even begun to fight, which gave me an even greater reason to relentlessly pursue justice for her.

The reporter didn't mention that Hope and Amber were in the same grade, that the only reason they could even mention Hope's name was that she celebrated her seventeenth birthday on the day of the shooting. She also failed to mention that Hope's sixteen-year-old friend had pulled the trigger and had stolen the car and taken Hope along for the ride.

While reading the news article, I couldn't get my mind off how Hope had ended our conversation. Why would Amber want Henry Esposito to be dead and what motivated her to pull the trigger to make it happen? What was in it for the teenager who Esposito and his friends were paying hundreds of dollars per week? Was she just sick of Esposito farming her out to his friends?

My phone rang. It was from a number I did not recognize. Most times I simply ignore those calls, thinking if the caller wanted to reach me, they would leave a voicemail. This time I picked up the phone and heard a female voice.

"Ms. Sanchez, this is Sergeant Costello with the Dallas Police Department. The district attorney's office asked me to reach out to you and tell you what we found on Henry Esposito's computer."

"Hope told me that Esposito took photographs and shot video of Amber and her. Do you have a video of the shooting?" I asked.

"We didn't find any photos or video. If he took photos or shot video that day, someone permanently erased the photos and video before we got there. His computers were wiped clean."

"Who could have gotten to Esposito's condo before the police?" I asked.

"I don't know. We haven't had a forensics expert look into whether a video was deleted."

Hope had told me that Esposito had frequently taken photos and shot video of Amber and her engaging with each other and playing with a revolver. But for some reason, he had not taken photos the day he was shot. *Did Esposito erase the photos?*

I asked Sergeant Costello if there was other evidence that Esposito had been molesting girls.

Costello didn't reply at first. I thought she must be weighing whether she should answer my question.

"A mother of a fifteen-year-old called a few months ago to report that she had found hundred-dollar bills in her daughter's wallet, and when she asked her daughter how she had gotten the money, the daughter reluctantly told her Henry Esposito had given her money each week to have sex with one of his friends."

"Why didn't the police arrest Esposito for statutory rape?" I asked.

"We started a detailed investigation. We got the name of Esposito's friend and started negotiating with his lawyer for him to plead guilty and provide evidence against Esposito. At that we were told the FBI had taken the case from us. After that I heard that the daughter had made up the story. I believe someone made a big payment to the girl and her mother."

"But the FBI had enough evidence to continue the investigation."

"They did, and Esposito knew that. We turned over what we had to the FBI and awaited word that the FBI arrested Esposito."

"What happened?"

"I was told that the girls the FBI interviewed all denied Esposito had trafficked them. We assumed they liked being able to buy upscale clothes, shoes, and electronic gadgets. I don't think the FBI had done much of anything by the time your client and her friend shot Esposito. I think Esposito had connections that slow-walked the investigation."

"Did the girl's mother tell you who paid her to keep her daughter's mouth shut?"

"No, we just assumed that Esposito, his lawyer, or one of his friends had paid the mother and daughter to withdraw the complaint."

"What happened to Esposito's friend who was ready to take a plea deal?"

"After Esposito was shot, he had less to give us for the plea deal and we had less evidence to convict him since the girl had recanted on her story."

"Can you tell me the name of Esposito's friend?"

"I can't tell you. I don't know his name. The only thing I know is that he is a lawyer with one of the prominent law firms in town. I believe the firm may have represented Esposito."

I was known for being blunt, and this would be one of those times. "If the Dallas PD had arrested Esposito, Hope Riley wouldn't be sitting in jail facing a murder charge."

"I know. I wanted to arrest him. I'm sorry. I was overruled because we didn't have enough evidence."

"Is it possible that Esposito erased the photos or that someone got to the crime scene before the police and destroyed the evidence on his computer?"

"I don't know. I never considered that possibility."

"May I ask you one more thing?"

"Sure."

"Did you find any photos or other evidence on Hope's cell phone?"

"You'll need to ask the district attorney."

I wanted to see it, but I decided to first ask Hope what was on her cell phone.

After my conversation with Sergeant Costello, I set up a meeting with Hope to find out what she thought may have been deleted from Esposito's computer and what, if anything, was on her cell phone.

Hope told me that, at first, Esposito had taken photos of her modeling clothes he had bought for her.

She said after a couple of weeks, he had taken photos of her in underwear as if she were a Victoria's Secret model. She said she had worn white in some photos and black with a garter belt and stockings in others.

She told me Esposito had later taken photos and video of her completely naked or in sexy lingerie and heels.

"You didn't object to him doing that?"

"No, I enjoyed it. You don't understand how it made me feel knowing I was pleasing him."

She was right. I most certainly didn't understand.

"Do you know if he took the same kind of photos and shot videos of other teenage girls?"

"Yes, he asked me to bring my friends to see him and he showed me photos of Amber and some other girls I didn't know. He also took photos and shot video of Amber and me naked together. He especially liked it when we were sexually arousing each other."

I could not believe a seventeen-year-old girl could be so nonchalant about Esposito abusing her and her friend.

"You never told Esposito what he was doing was wrong, or that he should stop taking photos and shooting videos of you?"

"No. A couple of times after we had sex, Mr. Esposito told me it could never happen again. But I knew he would want to the next time we were together. It was my choice. I could have said stop any time and he would have stopped."

"Did he ever give you drugs or alcohol?"

"No."

If Emma Riley or Father Michael knew that Esposito wasn't pursuing Hope as much as Hope was pursuing him, they'd be shocked. I suspected the district attorney would claim that Hope was less a victim and more an underage prostitute.

Christopher and Daniel had to know Esposito was exploiting teenage girls. I planned to ask Daniel next time they were together and make sure he told me what he knew. Did he and Christopher participate? If Daniel's law firm hadn't delayed Esposito's arrest, Hope wouldn't be stuck in the Dallas County Jail, awaiting a trial for murder, grand theft, and trafficking.

Esposito's wife had to know. That had to have been the reason she divorced him. What had he agreed to in the divorce settlement? Why didn't she encourage the police to arrest her ex-husband for abusing teenage girls?

Esposito had clearly taken advantage of Hope. He had manipulated and brainwashed Hope and she worshipped him, but she had actively participated and seemed to enjoy the charismatic man's attention. Esposito had known that at fifteen when he first had sex with Hope, she was incapable of consenting.

Hope and Amber didn't act like victims, or like they wanted to kill him because he had abused them and let his friends abuse Amber. Hope had more than once told me that she was flattered and excited by Esposito's attention. That statement made my task defending her extremely difficult. Even now Hope could not see herself as a victim. She was still proud that a rich, grown man had desired her.

I wanted to find out more about Hope, so I called Hope's school and arranged a time that afternoon to interview her female teachers. When I met with a group of teachers, one told me Hope had been a good student, with a boyfriend, until this past fall when her grades started slipping. I knew she had been a good student and I remembered she had dumped the boyfriend after the talent show.

No one knew what had happened with the boyfriend. Her teachers confirmed what Emma Riley had told me about Hope seeking attention and approval, especially from boys and male teachers. They showed me photos from the school yearbooks. Hope had become a young woman in less than a school year.

"Hope is introverted, except when she is performing. On stage she was extraordinarily talented, vibrant, and made a connection with the audience I had never seen from a high school student before," her music teacher said. "But I thought something changed after the talent show her sophomore year."

"What changed?"

"She got an opportunity to perform in a movie, and after that she seemed less interested in performing at school and more interested in getting parts in other movies. As a result, her grades started slipping."

Did any of you ask Hope how she got the part and what was going on?" I asked.

"I did," a young teacher replied. "She smiled when I asked her and said she had made a breakthrough with an agent."

"I knew Hope was working to pay for acting, voice, and modeling coaching, but I was worried she might be prostituting herself," an older teacher said."

That took me by surprise.

"What made you think she was prostituting herself?" I asked.

"Hope is not a good liar. When I asked her why she had stopped participating in after-school activities, she said she was modeling to earn money and help her mother. There was something about the way she responded that made me think there was more to the story."

I stared at the teacher, implying I couldn't believe she didn't pursue what she thought was more to the story.

"Ms. Roman, Hope was a victim, not a prostitute. Henry Esposito victimized her starting when she was merely fifteen years old."

The teacher leaned away from me, clearly embarrassed by her failure to find out more about how Hope was helping her mother.

"I'm sorry Ms. Sanchez. You're right."

"Did you know Hope had some learning disabilities?" a third teacher asked. "When she was in grade school, her classmates made fun of her. I think that experience impacted her. I believe she still feels like an outsider and has struggled because she lacks a father. She volunteered to tutor elementary school special education students after school."

"That all changed when I noticed that Hope and Amber had become inseparable," she remarked. "They had always been friends, but there was something different. I read in the news that Hope has been charged with trafficking and solicitation of a minor. How under the law does one girl get accused of trafficking and soliciting a girl in her class who is her best friend?"

"It's complicated," I replied. "What can you tell me about Amber?"

"Probably not much that you don't already know. I'm not sure it is appropriate for me to tell you anything."

"I suspect I can find out whatever you tell me, but it would be helpful to hear it from you."

"Amber has been written up for lying several times. She was labeled a slut when she broke up with a boyfriend and he leaked nude photos and videos she had shared with him. I was told she created an account advertising her availability on Backpage. I guarantee you that Amber persuaded Hope to help her get paid for sex by older men."

I had reached that same conclusion, but I wanted to know why the teacher believed it to be so.

"What has she lied about?" I asked.

"Many things. If she doesn't have her homework completed, there's always a reason. When she was caught cheating, and when she was caught stealing from another student, she denied it."

"What makes you think she asked Hope to help her get paid for sex?" I asked.

"Whenever the two of them are together, it is always Amber taking the lead. Hope is a follower, not a leader."

One of the other teachers spoke up. "Amber has had a difficult life with a mother in prison on drug charges and a father who abandoned her. She and her brother have been in foster care ever since. With no mother or father, she believes life is unfair and she should have what other students have, namely money for tech devices, clothes, and other things."

"Is there anything else I should know?" I asked.

"Yes, Amber kept a journal or diary. I saw her writing in it during class one day."

Hearing about the diary was the most important thing they told me. I wanted to find a way to see what she wrote in it.

"That's very helpful. Thank you all for taking time to meet with me."

I have to get the journal without Amber knowing I've seen it.

CHAPTER 13

Gabriela

Daniel helped me get an appointment with Esposito's two business partners. I hoped they might know if he had any enemies and share with me what they knew about his abusing underage teenage girls.

After going out for my morning run and drinking my first cup of coffee, I met Daniel at the Noble building and took the elevator up to the seventeenth floor, where we were greeted by a young, stylish receptionist. Daniel introduced Rhonda Williams, and as Rhonda escorted us to the conference room, I caught Daniel eyeing Rhonda's curvaceous behind.

While we waited in the conference room, I asked Daniel what he knew about Esposito's solicitation of minors for sex. Daniel denied knowing anything and told me that he had never seen Esposito with young girls.

Before I could ask the next question, two men dressed in fancy custom dress shirts, striped ties, and suit pants came into the room. One of the men had a shaved head, was clearly in great physical shape, and stood at least six inches taller than the other man, who had wavy gray hair, was overweight, and could barely keep up with his partner.

Turning to the taller, in-shape man, Daniel said, "Gabriela, this is James Hutton and Robert Gibbs. They were Henry Esposito's partners. Jim, Bob, Gabriela is defending a seventeen-year-old who is one of Henry's accused killers."

"The young girl I am defending did not kill Henry Esposito. She didn't even shoot his gun or know it was loaded," I told the two partners. "She's a victim and she should be released."

"That girl is no victim. She brought her friend to Henry's apartment and set the whole thing up. Then she stole Henry's car and fled," Hutton said. "She's as guilty as her friend who pulled the trigger."

I decided not to respond to his point. Instead, I asked, "What can you tell me about Mr. Esposito?"

"What do you want to know?" Gibbs asked.

"Did he have any enemies?"

"You mean other than your client and her girlfriend?"

"Yes, were there any clients or competitors who wanted him dead?"

"Our clients loved Henry," Hutton said. "He made a lot of money for them."

"Did either of you know he was having sex with underage girls?"

Hutton first looked at Gibbs. Then he turned and shook his head. "No, it never dawned on us and there is nothing that makes us believe that happened."

"I've seen a photo of the two of you, Esposito and my client."

"Ms. Sanchez, had you done some research you would have found that photo was taken at a charity event our firm sponsored," Gibbs said. "Your client was one of the scholarship candidates. There are photos of us with each of the candidates. Now, you've taken enough of our time today, I will ask Ms. Williams to escort you out."

"Before we go, I want to learn one more thing from you."

"What's that?" Gibbs asked.

"I know Henry Esposito entertained some of the top businessmen in Dallas at his apartment. Did you know any of the other men your partner allowed to molest young girls? Clearly those men had to be worried when the police were closing in on Henry Esposito."

"No, Ms. Sanchez. It's time for us to get back to work," Gibbs replied with his arms crossed at his chest. *You aren't good at covering a lie. Was Gibbs also molesting teenage girls?*

On their way down the hall, Rhonda Williams touched my arm and gestured me to let Daniel go ahead.

"Daniel, I need a couple of minutes down the hall. Will you get the car and I'll meet you in front of the building?"

"Sure."

When we entered the ladies' room, Rhonda looked to make sure we were alone.

"Ms. Sanchez, when Mr. and Ms. Esposito divorced, he bought a five-million-dollar insurance policy with Ms. Esposito the beneficiary as part of the divorce settlement. He planned to leave the majority of his estate in a trust for the children to keep his ex-wife from spending his money. Darla had five million reasons to prefer him to be dead rather than alive."

I don't normally jump to assumptions, but I was betting Esposito was more than just Rhonda's boss. I wanted her to keep talking, so I kept the thought to myself.

"I understand, but Esposito's ex-wife would have had to make an arrangement with Amber to kill him and know that Esposito would hand her a loaded gun. It seems like quite a stretch."

"It probably is, but nonetheless, it could have happened. She is not the only one who wanted him gone."

"What?"

"Mr. Hutton and Mr. Gibbs knew the police had started an investigation of Henry's relationships with underage girls. They wanted him to leave the partnership and he refused. If he left, he would have taken his clients with him. Now that he is dead, they inherited his clients."

They had lied to me.

"I see," I replied.

"Why are you telling me this?"

"Mr. Hutton and Mr. Gibbs are greedy men who have no respect for me or other women. Henry may have had a penchant for young women, but he always treated me with respect."

"Thank you, Ms. Williams."

In the car, Daniel scolded me for insinuating that Hudson and Gibbs knew of Esposito's exploitation of teenage girls. It was the first time I started to question my relationship with him.

"You should have asked them about the photo instead of jumping to a conclusion."

"Daniel, first, I did ask them, and I didn't jump to a conclusion. Second, I find it hard to believe that the people who knew Henry Esposito best, including his partners, you, and Christopher Duval, didn't put two and two together, or at the very least suspect something and ask him."

"Those men are our firm clients. You treated them like child molesters. I really wish you had not taken this case. No good will come out of you defending this teenager."

I noted that Daniel had not answered whether he or Christopher Duval knew what Henry Esposito was up to, and that made me concerned they had participated.

In a carefully controlled tone, I replied, "Henry Esposito was also your firm's client. If he was alive, I would have treated him like the pervert he was. Those men knew exactly what their partner was doing. Esposito didn't make any big effort to keep what he was doing secret."

Daniel was silent. That convinced me he knew Esposito had been exploiting teenage girls and he had done nothing to stop him. I wanted to ask if he had participated, but I decided not to confront him.

***

When I returned to the office, I called Esposito's ex-wife.

"Ms. Esposito, this is Gabriela Sanchez."

"Who?"

"Gabriela Sanchez. I am a lawyer and I represent Hope Riley."

"One of the girls who killed my ex-husband."

"She didn't kill him, Ms. Esposito. She was there when it happened, but her friend Amber Davis shot your ex-husband. May I come by and visit with you? I have some questions."

To my surprise, she agreed to meet with me that evening. I thought she might try some neuro linguistic programming technique on me.

After I sat down on her couch, Darla asked, "What is it you want to know?"

"I am trying to figure out who had a motive to kill your husband, and also how his loaded gun ended up in the hands of a teenage girl."

Darla's eyes hardened and she clenched her jaw. I knew she wouldn't help me. I was more interested in sizing up what kind of witness Darla would make at the trial.

"No one wanted to kill Henry other than the girl you are defending and her girlfriend," she replied. "They stole his money and his car and took off for Miami."

I decided to change the subject.

"Do you have any idea why your ex-husband wanted to take photos and videos of the girls with one of his guns?"

Darla lost the mean look, at least for a moment. "That doesn't surprise me. He took photos and shot videos of me holding his guns. He collected action figure photos of me holding guns. Let me show you some of them."

She invited me over to her computer. When she opened a folder, I saw several photos of Darla. In one she was wearing a black sports bra and black tights with her arms extended, holding a pistol. In another photo, Darla wore a black slit dress so one leg was showing and black gloves to her elbows. In this photo, she was pointing the pistol in the air. In another photo, she was on one knee in a black dress and black boots, holding what she told me was an AK-47. We spent the next ten minutes going over photos and videos Esposito had taken of Darla.

"I don't get it," I said. "The photos and videos are sexy, but I don't understand your ex-husband's fascination with near-naked women holding guns."

"It took me by surprise when he first told me. Then I found all kinds of videos on YouTube. There was a news segment about porn stars shooting guns."

I shook my head, still trying to figure out the erotic appeal of a half-naked or totally naked woman holding a gun.

"Henry made sure the guns were never loaded. One of those girls must have loaded the gun and shot him, took his money they found, and hit the road for Miami in his BMW."

"They took some money they found and drove your ex-husband's BMW toward Miami, but he was the one who was turned on by half-dressed girls pointing a gun. Is it possible your ex-husband didn't know it was loaded?"

"He collected guns. He would have known which of his guns were loaded and which ones were not."

"Ms. Esposito, did you discover your ex-husband was exploiting young girls, including Hope Riley?"

"Ms. Sanchez, has it ever occurred to you that your client may have seduced my ex-husband?"

"What would make you think that?"

"Because I seduced him, and it was very easy. I'm not sure you know much about men, Ms. Sanchez. My ex-husband, and just about every other man his age, like younger women because they look up to them, listen to them, hang on their every word, and think they are impressive. Henry believed talented people can change the world. That is why he supported the Dallas High School for the Performing Arts."

I was reeling from what she had said. Darla Esposito had blamed the victim. Would the jury blame Hope also? They might if they believed Darla.

I finally replied. "If what you say is true, then your ex-husband should have rejected Hope's advances and told her it wasn't right."

"Look at your client. She's far more mature than her age and looks like an adult, not like a teenager."

"And you knew he was seeing Hope?"

"I can't say because of the divorce settlement."

"Then I will take it you knew what he was doing and prefer not to talk about it."

"You can take it any way you want, but under the terms of our divorce decree I agreed to not make public the reasons for our divorce."

"He's dead, Ms. Esposito. There is no reason to keep what prompted the divorce secret."

"You would need to speak to my attorney about that," she replied.

I didn't want to speak to her attorney because I felt he would want his client to keep quiet. I went on with questions.

"Did you know your ex-husband promised to help Hope with a modeling and acting career and promised to pay for her to go to college?"

"I didn't know, but I am not surprised. He had connections with modeling agencies and Hollywood producers and agents. He started a scholarship program where his firm sponsored one or more candidates each year. Henry helped a lot of kids who needed his financial help or access to his connections."

"Hope had no motive for your ex-husband to die. He was helping her with her future career."

"Ms. Sanchez, has your client told you that Henry attempted to revise his will with a handwritten will and attempted to leave your client five hundred thousand dollars? He didn't leave me anything, but he left your client five hundred thousand dollars. That's more money than she might make in her entire life. Don't you think the money would give your client and her friend ample motive to kill my ex-husband?"

I stopped to catch my breath, trying to process what I had just heard.

"Hope Riley didn't know Esposito was leaving her money, and to the best of my knowledge, she still doesn't know. I've talked to her. She is distraught over your ex-husband's death."

"I plan to contest Henry's will since your client is charged with killing him. Fortunately, he didn't sign it, so I've been told it is not valid."

I decided to change the subject.

"Did you know that before he died, the police were investigating his abuse of teenage girls?" I asked.

"That's another subject I prefer not to discuss with you. I will simply say that before he was killed, I knew he was upset about something."

"Ms. Esposito, I was told your divorce settlement included your ex-husband buying a five-million-dollar life insurance policy. Is that correct?"

"Yes, it was Henry's idea to make sure I would be okay in the event he died. Both his father and mother had cancer and he was afraid he would die from cancer. You are not insinuating—"

"No, I am not insinuating anything. Were the kids the beneficiaries of the policy?"

"No, Henry trusted me to take care of them. I was the beneficiary."

"Have you notified the insurance company of his passing?"

"Yes."

I knew right then that Darla was going to be a formidable witness to cross-examine. She would place the blame on Hope for her marriage failing and would claim Hope wanted her husband to die so she could receive money he left her in his will. She would use every psychological technique in her arsenal to come across as the grieving widow and mother.

I asked if she knew which of her ex-husband's friends were having sex with underage girls he was providing them.

"Ms. Sanchez, my ex-husband led a double life. Everyone he met loved him. He had a way with people that I have never seen in another man. But, he and other powerful men had a thing for teenage girls that I am sure they did not want to be made public. Have you considered the other Dallas men who were molesting teenage girls? If they knew the police were closing in on Henry, one of them might have had good reason to want him gone."

That last answer was more information than I expected, given her reluctance to talk about her husband's misdeeds. But there was one thing I still didn't understand.

Why does a man married to one of the most beautiful women in Dallas have a sexual relationship with a girl not much older than his own daughters? Why does the same man have a fetish getting excited by naked and near-naked girls holding guns?

When I got home and did a search, I found photos and videos of girls holding guns, I even found a scholarly article discussing all the examples and why the writer believed some men find it erotic. Henry Esposito was one weird dude. He loved teenage girls and guns.

My father once told me that means, motive, and opportunity were the summation of solving and prosecuting a crime. Sadly, so far, under Texas law, Hope was the only person who met the test for all three. Several others had a motive, but how could I show they had the means or opportunity?

Chapter 14

Gabriela

I had looked forward to going home for Christmas for some time, even though I could only spend a few days. I planned to arrive on December the twenty-third and spend the next two days with my family. I made a commitment to meet with Congressman Moreno for breakfast on Thursday, the day after Christmas. That was an important meeting for me because I hoped to decide whether to accept his invitation to run for his congressional seat.

At five-thirty that evening, I stepped off the curb at the McAllen airport and got in the passenger side of my father's car. My mother sat in the back seat.

As we pulled away from the curb, my father turned and said, "I should have had a doorman open the car door for you, since you will be our next congressional representative."

I turned and looked my mother. Her smile turned into an agonized frown, and that told me all I needed to know about her feelings.

"This is no time to be joking, Papá. I need your thoughts on whether I should run for Congressman Moreno's seat."

He knew I really wasn't looking for his advice. He asked, "Isn't that something you have to decide on your own?" he asked.

"Yes, but I always want your and Mama's thoughts before I decide."

I turned and looked back at Mama and her face hadn't changed.

Instead of giving me advice, he asked me a series of questions designed to help me make up my own mind.

I spent all day Christmas Day visiting with my brothers and their children and my grandmother, who we picked up at the assisted living facility. Each of my nephews and nieces showed me their latest gadgets they had received for Christmas. Thomas offered to let me ride on his new Razor Power Core Scooter. I declined.

I wanted to spend more time with my grandmother. From the time I was a little girl, I called my grandmother Nana, and even now I still call her Nana. At first, Nana didn't recognize me. Like her mother before her, Nana had lost her sight due to glaucoma. When she heard my voice, she leaned forward to give me a big hug. As I had anticipated, she asked if I had found a man to marry and I saw the disappointment when I told her I was still working on that.

When I was a young child in grade school, Nana and my great-grandmother lived together. They frequently took care of me after school. I remember play-acting that I was a teacher. Nana and my great-grandmother were my misbehaving pupils. On other occasions, I pl-ay-acted that I was a lawyer, like my father, and I cross-examined Nana and my great- grandmother. My great-grandmother passed away when I was nine. Nana asked me to speak at her funeral. It was the first time I spoke to a group in public. As I recalled our time together, I broke down. I finished my eulogy in tears. Seeing my grandmother in assisted living reminded me of those times together and that I would not see her very often if I remained in Dallas.

On Thursday morning I drove my father's car to Lupita's Café, a small family-owned restaurant where the locals meet for breakfast or lunch. Even though it was a workday, patrons were seated at every table, and a line of people waited outside. Luis Moreno was seated at a table surrounded by well-wishers and the restaurant staff.

Like many locally owned Mexican restaurants in the Valley, Lupita's was known for its large homemade flour tortillas and its homemade tamales. I had never found any better in Dallas. I ordered two pork tamales and coffee. Moreno spent the next fifteen minutes talking to each of his constituents who came by the table. I thought this was one part of being a congresswoman I would hate. I prefer eating breakfast and drinking my coffee alone.

Finally, Moreno turned his attention to me, and with a big smile gave me a hug.

I started back with my protests about his retiring. He said he had grown tired of politics in Washington and the progressives had threatened to primary him.

He acknowledged that he thought I was a good candidate to replace him because I was young, a woman, and had grown up in the Valley. He surprised me by saying President Trump was resonating with the local voters and that was one reason a new face was needed.

A constituent came to our table and asked the congressman a question. After the congressman had answered, I told him I appreciated his honesty, but I thought it was identity politics and there must be women who stayed in the Valley who would be a better fit.

Congressman Moreno tried to smooth things over. He waved his arm with his palm up while telling me that none of the women here had my magnetic personality and worldview. He also claimed that my trial experience had toughened me for the fights I would face in Washington.

"I don't want to get into fights in Washington. I'm tired of watching partisan bickering and members of Congress who show up for interviews with their talking points."

"I'm tired of that also. You can change Washington."

I laughed out loud, remembering when the younger Bush ran for president and claimed he would be able to reach across the aisle.

"Congressman, it's too late to change Washington. It's broken beyond repair, and one representative from the Rio Grande Valley can't put it back together. Plus, I have experience in the courtroom and no experience in the Capitol building."

Congressman Moreno sensed he had not convinced me. Before I knew it, the congressman stood on his chair, clapped his hands until everyone in Lupita's stopped talking.

"I want those of you who don't know her to come speak to Gabriela Sanchez. I am considering retiring from Congress, but only if I can make sure you, your family, and friends will be represented by someone I know who will care about you. Gabriela Sanchez is that person."

He asked me to stand on a chair next to him. People started cheering for me. When we both sat down, people started coming by to meet me. I spent the next three hours listening to each person who came by my table. I learned they were most interested in jobs and the economy and that their values focused on family.

I had to admit I liked the interaction.

He asked what work I had left to be done in Dallas and I told him I was defending a teenage girl accused of killing Henry Esposito. I said her trial was scheduled for early March and I hoped I could get the cased dismissed before the trial.

"Esposito, the Dallas investment banker?" he asked.

"Yes, did you know him?"

"He has been a major contributor to the Democratic Party."

I thought he would ask me to drop the case. To my surprise, he encouraged me to defend her.

He asked, "How did a seventeen-year-old girl even know Esposito?"

"The priest told me Esposito was having sex with her and with other girls."

"Oh my. I want you to take on her defense. Stopping trafficking of young girls is an important cause here and throughout Texas. Your potential voters will applaud you for representing a teenage girl who was trafficked. I will make sure they know what you are doing."

"Even if she is not Hispanic?"

"Yes, but you must successfully defend her. Losing her case would probably hurt your election chances."

Just what I needed—more pressure. I hated losing. I feared losing, and in this case, I knew I would face even greater pressure than the Duval trial because a young girl's future was on the line. Now, Moreno had added even more pressure. The stakes were getting higher by the minute.

"No pressure, right?"

"You face pressure on any case you undertake. No more pressure than normal. Just make sure you are finished and able to come home in March."

I decided to run for Congressman Moreno's seat. I came back to Dallas with two goals: First, I wanted—no I needed—to resolve Hope's case by the end of the trial in early March. Second, I still wanted and needed to find the defense that would persuade the jury Hope was not guilty. I was almost certain Hope's trial would be done by early March. I had still not figured out her best defense, and the trial was right around the corner.

February 2020

CHAPTER 15

Gabriela

Time flew by and I was preparing for the trial in March and enjoying unusually warm weather.

On a warm Sunday in February, I was outside walking my dog, Bella, when I came across a young family walking on the sidewalk. A young boy who appeared to be maybe four or five years old approached me with his hand out to pet Bella. I looked at the boy and said, "This is Bella, would you like to pet her?"

As the young boy reached out for Bella, the father grabbed him from behind and said, "He doesn't want to pet your dog."

I pulled Bella back, stunned by the father's words. I had never experienced a parent who didn't want his or her child to pet Bella. As I walked away, I looked back, still wondering if I had done anything that caused the father to pull his young son back. When I got home, I turned on my television. Among the news stories was one about the World Health Organization declaring a public health emergency for only the sixth time. It was called the Coronavirus.

I didn't know what to make of the announcement, but I thought that may have somehow been why the father pulled his son away from Bella. I sent a text to my brother, Luis, sharing the story and that it might be the new normal as a result of the public health emergency. Luis had not heard of the virus and asked if it had anything to do with the beer. I laughed.

Afterward, having no idea how what I had seen on television would impact me or my representation of Hope, I forgot about it and set out in my car to pick up my father at the airport.

"Why are you spending time investigating who might have had a reason to want Esposito to be dead?" my father asked.

"Papá, I have to find Hope's best defense to the murder charge."

"She didn't know the gun was loaded. She didn't pull the trigger. She wasn't even in the same room when the first shot was fired. She had every reason to want Henry Esposito to stay alive. He had already secured a modeling job for her and a bit part in a movie, and he had promised to pay for college and do more to help her with an acting and modeling career. Isn't that her best defense?"

"It might be, Papá, but if Amber testifies that Hope told her by nodding to pull the trigger, I need to piece together why Amber really pulled the trigger. I don't think it was because Esposito was abusing her."

"I can imagine several people wanted Esposito dead, but it's a stretch to say that someone managed to have a sixteen-year-old girl kill Esposito. He or she had to find Hope Riley and Amber Davis and know they both were having sex with Esposito. Then that person would have to persuade one or both to kill him. Then Amber would have to wait until the day when Esposito handed her a loaded revolver. Then while Esposito was lying down on his stomach, Amber would have had to pull the trigger three times to make sure Esposito was dead. Suppose you spend precious time, and you find out all of those things. I'm not sure how that will be Hope's best defense."

"Papá, they've also charged Hope with human trafficking and contributing to the exploitation of a minor."

"How could that be? Esposito was the trafficker. Hope was a victim, not a trafficker."

"I know that, but Hope doesn't think she was victimized. She told me she loved Esposito because he was the first boy or man who made her feel cared for."

"He manipulated her by acting like he cared and promising her a career in modeling and acting. She told us he introduced her to a Hollywood agent and professional photographer. She was just a kid. She didn't know he was exploiting her. He was also exploiting her friends. She had to know she wasn't the only one."

"I know that. But I've been told Amber will testify that Hope recruited her to be one of Esposito's girls and that Esposito had sex with her when Hope was there."

"She may have done that to help her friend or to make her abuser happy. Has a date been set for the trial?"

"Yes, Monday, March thirtieth."

"You have a few weeks to find out what happened. What has Hope told you about how Amber got involved?"

"Amber was living in a foster home and she had no money to buy anything for herself. She had been seeing men from an ad she put on Backpage before the government shut it down. Then she used Snapchat and Facebook messenger to meet men for sex. She saw Hope with one-hundred-dollar bills and asked how Hope had so much money, and Hope told her she was posing and having sex with Henry Esposito."

"Why did Hope tell her about Esposito?"

"I suppose because they were good friends from school and Amber bugged her to find out why suddenly she had some money.

Probably Hope and Amber had never seen one-hundred-dollar bills before."

"I'm sure Esposito and his friends were a higher class than men who found her on a Backpage ad."

I agreed.

At that point my father asked if I had decided about running for Congressman Moreno's seat.

"I told the congressman I wanted to run, but I could not file in time and only if no one would contest me in the primary. I have no time to campaign in the Valley for a primary in March just a few weeks before the trial."

"What did he say?"

"Not to worry about the filing deadline. To accommodate me he would announce his retirement at the end of his term after the filing deadline."

"Has anyone expressed interest in running against you?"

"No, Congressman Moreno says his seat is mine and I want to run and defeat the Republican challenger. He plans to announce his retirement and introduce me as his chosen successor as soon as Hope's trial is over."

I knew my father wanted me to come home. He said I had gone to Dallas to build a reputation and I had accomplished that. He claimed I would be home from Washington more often than I had been home from Dallas.

Everything was falling into place for me to return home and become a congresswoman.

Chapter 16

Gabriela

I turned my attention to successfully defending what I expected could be my last client. I spent the next day doing research on how I could get Hope released from jail. I thought about asking once again for the judge to reduce the one-million-dollar bail. That hadn't worked the first time and I doubted raising the issue a second time would change the judge's mind.

After some research, I discovered celebrities had exerted mass public pressure for the release of other girls who, after becoming victims of sexual abuse had shot and killed a predator. I hoped one or more of those celebrities would get behind Hope and raise money for her bail, or at least bring her case to the attention of the public. I needed to raise one hundred thousand dollars for the cash needed for a one-million-dollar bail bond.

I was no social media expert, and I had been the victim of a social media campaign when I defended Sparks Duval, but after more research, I started a GoFundMe page for Hope. Then, using the Twitter account that the PR firm had set up for me during the Duval defense, I started tweeting with the hashtag #freeHope.

My next step was to reconnect with the television reporters who had interviewed me during the Duval trial. When I told them Hope's story, many agreed to let me appear on their television news shows. On one Sunday, I was booked on three weekly news shows, during which I was able to describe how bad it was in Texas for a seventeen-year-old girl awaiting trial to be stuck in what could be described as solitary confinement in a cell no bigger than a closet with a bench for a bed.

One reporter asked, "Why does Texas treat seventeen-year-old boys and girls as adults?"

"That's a great question," I replied. "I was shocked when I learned that it has been that way for a long time. Over the last eight years, bills have been introduced in the Texas legislature to change the law and none have been passed."

"How does this law affect Hope Riley?"

"It affects her in more ways than you can possibly imagine. Instead of making an effort to rehabilitate Hope, the state seeks to incarcerate her. Instead of being able to continue her education, Hope is locked up in a claustrophobic cell for up to twenty-three hours a day. She only sees corrections officers. This isolation, while designed to protect the teenagers from other inmates, potentially causes severe damage to their physical and mental health. I have witnessed it in Hope just in the short time she has been in jail."

"Why was she featured in the news and her friend was not?" I was asked. I had planted that question. I wanted the world to know that in Texas she had been treated as an adult only because her friend shot Esposito on her birthday. Sadly, even if a jury found her not guilty, her life would be changed forever while her friend's record would be kept confidential. That seemed to grab the media's attention.

"Why hasn't Texas changed its law?" a reporter asked.

"I wish I knew the answer," I replied. "The sheriffs who run the jails have sought to have the law changed because they must house the seventeen-year-old inmates separately from the general population. It costs Dallas County over four million dollars a year to separately house seventeen-year-old girls and boys."

"Why does Hope have to wait in jail for her trial?"

"Because the judge set her bail at a sum well beyond her mother's ability to pay. If she had grown up in north Dallas, her family would most likely have the money to make her bail. We are trying to raise the money so she can be out on bail and continue her schooling before the trial."

"And tell our viewers when Hope's trial will be."

"It will be on Monday the thirtieth of March."

"I have one more question," a reporter said. There are rumors that Henry Esposito deleted hundreds of photos and videos of your client and other underage girls. Can you confirm that is true?"

I shook my head.

"I can't comment on that."

"Well, thank you Ms. Sanchez."

"Thank you for having me as a guest. Viewers who care about the safety of teenage girls should go to the 'Free Hope GoFundMe' page and contribute to our effort to raise money for her bail."

After getting Hope and Emily Riley's permission, on Twitter and on Facebook, I sent messages with jail house photos of Hope to several of the celebrities who had supported the release of other teenage trafficking victims. During the first week, not one of them replied. Why wouldn't they support Hope and help raise money for her bail?

I asked Father Michael to help raise money for Hope's bail. He said he couldn't raise money for one parishioner. The irony struck me. The parish could ask me to represent Hope for free, but it could not ask for money to help her with bail.

On Monday morning, the day after the television interview, Lucia came into my office, and in an excited voice said, "Judge Foster wants you to report to her courtroom this afternoon at two o'clock."

"Did she say why?"

"Robin Polk, the Hope Riley prosecutor, filed a motion to have Judge Foster enter a gag order, stopping you from speaking about the case in the news or social media. I put the motion on your desk."

I had hoped that the publicity would convince the Dallas DA to drop the charges against Hope. I was wrong.

Having never defended a case in the Dallas County Criminal Court, I didn't know anything about Robin Polk. I decided to do some research and talk to Dallas criminal lawyers.

I discovered Polk was forty-nine years old and had worked in the Dallas District Attorney's office for the last twenty years. Polk had prosecuted over one hundred jury cases, including dozens of murder cases.

She seemed to crave the media attention. I found at least a dozen articles about her. She was a frequent guest on cable news shows commenting on high-profile trials. One writer described Polk as the most tenacious prosecutor in Texas.

When I asked criminal defense attorneys, I learned they thought Polk was dishonest, unethical, and corrupt. They said she had convicted innocent defendants by hiding exculpatory evidence and making offers to jail house snitches to testify against defendants. They told me she was so driven to win each case that she ignored her obligations to seek justice.

When I mentioned that Hope was essentially in isolation so I didn't need to worry about her being accused of making a jailhouse confession, the lawyers told me to worry about what Polk would offer Amber Davis to testify against Hope. I made a note of that.

While we waited, Polk stood so she was staring down at me.

"Miss Sanchez, I don't know what brought you into a case I am prosecuting, but in case you haven't heard, I have never lost a murder case, and you can pretty much count on this case going to trial."

I wanted to say something like, "Well you've never tried a case against me." I decided to just bite my lip and keep my mouth shut, while knowing Polk would do anything to convict Hope and keep her perfect record in murder cases. Knowing Polk didn't play by the rules, I thought my best chance would be to convince her she might lose. If I could do that, she might drop the charges rather than take a chance in court.

At two o'clock, Robin Polk and I were escorted into Judge Foster's office.

"Ms. Sanchez, what in the world are you doing going on television? Ms. Polk has filed a motion to prohibit you from making a circus of this case. We don't permit pre-trial publicity to influence a jury in this court. Do you understand me?"

"Your Honor, I am representing a seventeen-year-old girl who is rotting in the Dallas County Jail just because the crime for which she is accused took place on her seventeenth birthday. You set her bail at one million dollars meaning she would need to post a one-hundred-thousand-dollar bond. Her mother has no money or property to post. I've been trying to raise money so she can post the bond and be released."

"Ms. Sanchez, I know all of that. I know you are new to this court, but even so, I didn't think it would be necessary for Ms. Polk to file a motion and for me to order you to not talk about the case. I am doing that now. I am issuing a gag order. You will not speak about the case or post anything on social media. Nor will you ask anyone else to speak on behalf of your client or post on behalf of your client. I will ask you one more time. Do you understand me now?"

I caught Polk smirking. *What a...*

"Yes, Your Honor. You should reduce Hope's bail. Neither she nor her mother have any money for bail."

"No, Ms. Sanchez. If they don't have any money, reducing bail won't make a difference. More importantly, your client is a flight risk. She fled after the shooting. I don't want her to have another opportunity."

When I looked at the GoFundMe page, I saw the amount contributed was slightly under ten thousand dollars. That wasn't a good sign. I pondered who I might ask to promote the page.

I had hoped I could make the public aware of Hope's plight and that donors would contribute to her bail bond. Instead, the judge who would set the amount of her bail and preside over her trial seemed to be already against her. Plus, I learned that Robin Polk was hell-bent on convicting Hope and not afraid of crossing the ethical line to do so.

When a lawyer is going up against an unethical prosecutor and has drawn an unfair judge, all she has left to save her client's freedom is the jury.

March 2020

CHAPTER 17

Gabriela

I met Daniel in a busy, upscale Plano Tex-Mex restaurant on Saturday night in early March. Daniel had chosen the restaurant because he wanted to discuss our planned trip to Cabo San Lucas in the middle of April after I defended Hope Riley. I had not told him that I had already canceled the trip because I would be campaigning for Congress back home.

I had never eaten or shopped in the area off the toll road near the new Cowboys headquarters. It was further north than my normal drive to eat. When I turned on the main street, I was surprised by the size of the crowd. I was especially surprised by the number of people in their early twenties walking along the street. I had not known this area was such a happening spot.

Daniel had told me to valet park my car rather than use one of the parking garages. After handing my keys to the parking attendant,

I walked across the street into the wall-to-wall packed restaurant. It was so noisy in the restaurant that I could barely hear the young, well-dressed woman at the reception desk. I told her the reservation was in the name of Mr. Thompson. The young woman found it on her iPad and escorted me to a table for two where Daniel was sitting waiting.

I opened the menu and saw the various margarita offerings, and when the young waiter came by, I ordered one with jalapeño and citrus with Tajin seasoning on the rim. Daniel ordered a Pacifico beer with lime.

Over the next twenty minutes, I told Daniel I had canceled the trip to Cabo because I was considering campaigning for Congress in the Valley. He frowned and looked as if he had just seen his dog get hit by a car. He said very little during our dinner and I knew right then that he had decided it was time for him to move on.

After dinner we walked outside.

Before he had a chance to move on, I had a few questions.

"Daniel, I need to know more about Henry Esposito."

"You know I can't tell you what is covered by the lawyer–client privilege."

"He's dead. The privilege didn't necessarily follow him into his grave. Besides, I'm not asking for anything confidential he may have told you as his lawyer. I want to know more about what you know as one of his best friends."

"So, what do you want to know?" Daniel asked.

"Did he have enemies?"

"How many times have you asked that question? What kind of enemies?"

"The kind who might threaten him or want him dead."

"He had several enemies who might want to scare him and some who might even want him dead, but none that I know of would have persuaded a sixteen-year-old girl to pull the trigger."

"Give me an example," I said.

"Have you considered the possibility that your client or her friend may have had a boyfriend who wasn't happy that a forty-something-year-old man was screwing his girlfriend?"

I had dismissed Hope's boyfriend. Her teachers had mentioned the boyfriend, but they said he had quickly moved on to another girl. I hadn't thought he could be involved. I had no idea if Amber had a boyfriend.

"No. I haven't considered that possibility."

"Wouldn't a boyfriend of one of the girls have an inside chance to persuade his girlfriend to shoot Henry Esposito?"

"That's possible," I replied.

"A jilted boyfriend would certainly have a motive."

"A jilted boyfriend may have had a motive, but I can't see how he could orchestrate the events leading to Esposito's death."

I changed the subject. "Did you know Henry Esposito set up his underage girls with his friends?"

Daniel frowned and pursed his lips. "You think Henry set me up with one of his girls?"

I looked into his eyes, trying to see if he may have been one of those men. If he was, he didn't give me any visual clue.

"I didn't say that. I asked if you know of anyone Henry set up."

"Why?" Daniel asked.

"Because the police were closing an investigation and getting ready to arrest Henry Esposito. Any close friends would not have wanted Esposito to spill the beans on their participation in the child-trafficking. A friend of Esposito's who didn't want to be outed as a child molester would have known about his gun collection. He might have loaded one of Esposito's guns and told Amber Davis which gun was loaded."

"So how would this person pay her, and wouldn't he be afraid she would spill the beans to save herself? He'd more likely make sure Amber didn't survive while the police were looking for her."

"Not if the person set up a payment to Amber when she and Hope got to Miami."

"That sounds way too farfetched to be a likely possibility."

"They decided to go to Miami in Esposito's car. Amber suggested it and Hope went along. Amber had to have a reason for picking Miami."

He laughed it off, so I changed the subject.

"I've learned that Esposito trafficked Amber with his friends and even though she won't admit it, he may have trafficked Hope. Do you know if Christopher Duval was messing around with Esposito's underage girls?"

"No way. Christopher Duval can have any woman in Dallas he wants. Why would he mess around with high school girls? Did Hope tell you the names of any of Esposito's friends?"

I didn't mention that I knew from personal experience that Christopher could not have any woman in Dallas he wanted. But Daniel did have a point. Christopher seemed far more interested in women than teenage girls.

"You know I can't tell you what Hope has said to me, but why are you asking? Do you know anything more about his friends who might not want Esposito to be arrested?" I asked.

Daniel raised both of his arms in front of him and made fists. Then he blurted out.

"How many times do I need to tell you I know nothing that would help your defense. Can we just go to your place and have an after-dinner drink and relax with one another?"

"I'm sorry," I said. "I'm tired from trying to speak above the noise in that restaurant. I just want to go home alone and chill. I think we should take a break from each other until I finish with Hope's case."

"A break from each other, why?"

"Your firm represented Esposito. Your firm represents his estate. We have a conflict of interests until this case is over."

"Would you be willing to have dinner next weekend and see if we can deal with what you believe is a conflict?"

"I doubt you can convince me. Plus, Hope's trial will be finished in March and then I am moving back home to the Rio Grande Valley. I don't see much of a future for us."

I smiled and handed my valet ticket to the attendant. I had hoped Daniel would help me and I was convinced he knew something.

He chose to put his dead high school classmate ahead of me. I went back to my condo knowing as challenging as defending Hope seemed to be, one way or another it would be over by the middle of March.

CHAPTER 18

Gabriela

I turned on the television and watched President Trump and the Coronavirus Task Force announce, "15 Days to Slow the Spread."

Damn, Damn, Damn. Those were among the many swear words I uttered even though no one could hear me.

I dialed Luis Moreno's secret cell phone number he had given me. I hoped he would understand what I was facing.

"Congressman, this is Gabriela. The trial has been postponed until June eighth and I'm not sure that there will be juries sitting even then."

As I had anticipated, he asked if I could enter into a plea deal and be done with the case.

I told him there was no way. When he protested, I said, "They've charged her with murder and Hope says she wasn't even in the same room, much less that her friend had a gun and planned to pull the trigger. They've also charged her with grand theft of Esposito's BMW and trafficking her friend Amber. The district attorney would deal if Hope identified other men who were abusing teenage girls, but unfortunately she doesn't know any of those men, or at least that is what she has told me."

Then he asked me to withdraw and tell the judge I was withdrawing to run for Congress. He said he was certain the judge would understand.

I truly wanted to represent the people who needed a voice a Congress, but I couldn't do it. I could not in good conscience abandon Hope now to satisfy myself.

"I'm sorry, really sorry, but I won't abandon Hope. She's counting on me. Her mother has put her faith in me. You might have to stay in Congress for another term or find someone who is not stuck with a trial that is delayed due to COVID-19."

I waited for his reply.

Finally, I heard him clear his throat. "Gabriela, if you finish with the trial in the week of June eighth, I believe you could still have enough time to campaign."

"I have no way of knowing if the trial will be over in that week. What if COVID delays the trial until July or August?"

"I'm deeply disappointed," the congressman replied. "But your decision has made me believe even more that I was right about you. I admire you. We never dreamed when we first talked that a world pandemic would stand in the way of you taking my seat in Congress."

What could I say? Moreno understood why I couldn't abandon a girl stuck in jail for a crime she witnessed but did not commit.

"Congressman Moreno, I pray the trial will be completed in June so I can come back home."

What else could go wrong in 2020? I thought I might wake up one day and find everything that had happened was part of a dream.

CHAPTER 19

Gabriela

I was wallowing in my own sorrow. I had never been in a situation where trials had to be postponed. I had no control over when the courts would reopen. Foster had postponed the trial until June, I couldn't see Hope, I couldn't speak to her, and the Dallas County judge had issued a shelter-in-place order, directing all Dallas County residents to stay in their homes. Hope was sitting in jail with no idea what had happened. I worried about her mental health.

I hoped someone at the jail had told her what had happened, and that she would have to be careful and patient. Since I really didn't understand what was going on, I was certain no one in the jail understood either.

I poured another glass of wine. I was going crazy being home with nothing to do. Essentially the only stores open were grocery stores and pharmacies. I had gone to the store and there was no toilet paper, no sanitizer, no meat. I couldn't work out because fitness clubs were closed. I couldn't get my hair cut because hair salons were closed, and I couldn't get my nails done because nail salons were closed.

I felt sorry for myself, being forced to shelter in place. But Hope was enduring far greater anxiety through isolation in a small cell for twenty-three hours a day at the jail.

In March I could play golf, but I couldn't play in Dallas County because the county judge shut down all parks and golf courses. In some counties, some courses were shut down. I had to walk at any of the courses that were open. I took my own water because there was no water on the courses, bathrooms were closed, the pins stayed in, there were no rakes for the bunkers. It was a different game.

I felt blessed to be able to get outside and do something rather than be stuck at home. I had it far better than Hope, who I worried would become so depressed that she would commit suicide.

At least we had a trial date, albeit three months later.

I was frantic to get her out of jail. I did some research and found a Texas statute titled: Release Because of Delay.

I discovered it essentially provides that if the state is not ready for trial in ninety days in a felony case, the defendant must be released either on a personal bond or reducing bail. I thought I could argue it applies during COVID trial delays.

I filed a motion to release Hope on her personal bond or reduce bail. I didn't expect Judge Foster to rule in my favor because she would not likely agree the statute applied to COVID. Two days later, Judge Foster's assistant called and told me Judge Foster would hear the motion by Zoom at ten o'clock the following morning.

The assistant told me that she would contact the sheriff's office so that Hope would be included in the Zoom hearing. I asked if I could have five minutes before the hearing to converse with my client before the hearing.

I was given the five minutes on Zoom with Hope the next morning and used our time alone to explain what was going on and why the hearing wasn't in a courtroom. When we talked about the trial being reset for June, Hope slumped in her chair and her lip trembled before she started to cry.

"I'm sorry Hope. I am doing everything I can to get you released on bail. The hearing today is to get you released on a personal bond, which is no bail, or at worst reduce your bail. I want you to think about how much your mother cares about you."

"Ms. Sanchez, I need the judge to release me with no bail. It doesn't matter how much the judge reduces the bail, my mother has no money and neither do I."

"Then let's hope the judge is willing to release you on a personal bond."

Hope's smiled and lifted her eyes. She was already focused on leaving the jail.

I was far less optimistic.

Chapter 20

Gabriela

Twenty minutes later, the Zoom hearing began. It was the first time I had argued a motion while staring at my computer. I desperately wanted Judge Foster to allow Hope to go home. I argued that the Texas statute required the court to release Hope on her personal bond.

Robin Polk argued that the statute was written to prevent prosecutors from indiscriminately delaying the trial of an incarcerated defendant. In this case, she argued, the state was ready to try Hope Riley at any time and the defendant Riley could go to trial with a jury using Zoom as they were doing for this hearing.

When I had a chance to pick up the argument, I replied, "Your Honor, Hope Riley is entitled to a live jury trial and she should not be forced to stay in what the newspapers have described as a 'petri dish for infection,' where the risk of Hope being infected is exponentially higher than in her home."

Polk countered, "Your Honor, the defendant is isolated on the sixth floor and never comes in contact with the general population."

Before she could continue, I said, "Your Honor, each prison guard or staff member who comes in contact with Hope, has been in contact with the general population and has been in contact with the world outside the jail."

"She is still a flight risk," Polk snapped, raising her voice.

"Your Honor, that's nonsense. First, she no longer has a passport. Second, travel outside of Texas is shut down during the pandemic."

"She can still leave the state. No one is checking at the state line and turning people back."

I jumped in again. "Your Honor, you could order that she have an ankle monitor and stay at home pursuant to the current shelter-in-place order."

Finally, Judge Foster spoke.

"Currently there can be no live trials until May eleventh. I have reset Ms. Riley's trial for June eighth. So, Ms. Riley doesn't have that much longer to wait. I am not inclined to release her on her own recognizance, but I will reduce her bail to one hundred thousand dollars, and she will be required to wear an ankle monitor. If that is all for today, the hearing is adjourned."

"Your Honor, before we conclude, I have a request," I said.

"What is that, Ms. Sanchez?"

"You have issued a gag order so I can't go on television or be interviewed by a newspaper reporter, or even go on social medial to say anything about Hope's case. I ask that you make an exception in your order that allows me to help raise funds for Hope's bail."

Polk immediately objected, claiming there was no way I could talk about Hope's bail without talking about the case and thus violating the gag order.

Judge Foster paused for a moment. "Ms. Sanchez, you may seek to raise money for your client's bail, but you may not argue your case in the media. Understood?"

"Yes, Your Honor."

With that, the camera on Judge Foster clicked off. When I looked at my computer screen, I saw Hope crying.

"Could I have a private moment with my client?" I asked.

When only the two of us were on the screen, I said, "Hope, we'll get the money for your bail. You'll be out in just a few days."

Judge Foster had reduced the bail to an amount that I was certain I could raise for her. Texas is the only state that permits a lawyer to post bond for his or her client. So, while arguably I could do it, most lawyers, including my father, believe it is unethical and creates conflicts of interest.

I expected Hope to have little or no knowledge of what the COVID rules were in Dallas. I planned to do my best to explain those rules to her.

Chapter 21

Gabriela

I have never been a fan of social media, but in this instance, I strategically used it by finding tweets and Facebook posts about other child-trafficked defendants and retweeting and reposting with a reference to Hope Riley. Within three days, we had raised more than thirty thousand dollars, and I paid a bail bondsman to post the bail for her.

I thought our problem was solved until I contacted the company that provides the ankle monitors for people out on bail. To my astonishment, I was told that none of their employees were willing to go into the Dallas County Jail to place the ankle monitor on a prisoner.

WTF

"They have nothing to worry about," I replied. "My client is in isolation from other prisoners, and she does not have the virus."

"That doesn't matter, our employee would have to get to where she is in isolation. Haven't you read the newspaper? Dallas County Jail is the epicenter of infections in Dallas."

Everything about Hope's case and about this year had blown my mind. But this topped it all. I had finally persuaded the judge to reduce the bail. Hope's mother had finally raised enough money to post the bond, and now Hope remained in jail because none of the ankle monitor employees would enter the jail. I had to do something, but what could I do?

"Would you be willing to allow me to take an ankle monitor and put it on my client in the jail?"

"If a judge orders us to allow you, we will. Short of that I say no."

To get a judge to order it would take at least another week with Hope stuck in isolation on the sixth floor.

When I told Hope during a Zoom conference, she started crying.

"I am all alone. I have no one to talk to. I can't take any classes. The guards tell me every day there's a good chance I will get COVID, and maybe die before I get out of here. I don't even know what COVID is, but the guards talk about it every day."

"Hope, things aren't going to be much better when you are released. A Dallas judge has ordered everyone in Dallas County to shelter in place. I don't believe kids will go back to school after spring break. You will be stuck at home."

"I will be happy to be at home with my mother."

"I'm sure your mother will be very happy to have you home with her."

Four days later, Judge Foster, Robin Polk and I were back together on a Zoom court hearing.

"Ms. Sanchez, you have moved the court to allow your client to be out on bail without an ankle monitor, or alternatively to order Cameron Company to allow you to install the ankle monitor on your client."

"Yes, Your Honor."

I expected Polk to oppose me, but when Judge Foster asked for her response, I was taken by surprise.

"Your Honor, if Ms. Sanchez's client is tested for COVID-19 before she is released on bail, the state has no objection to her release without an ankle monitor. I suspect that with the pandemic, Ms. Sanchez's client isn't going anywhere before her trial."

"Well, then with no objection by the state, I will allow Hope Riley to be out of jail on bond with no ankle monitor. Anything else before we adjourn?"

"Your Honor, can we keep the Zoom conference going after you leave so that I may speak with Ms. Sanchez?"

"You may." With that, the judge was no longer on the screen.

"May I call you Gabriela?" Polk asked.

"Sure," I replied.

"Gabriela, your client may have valuable information that would help us arrest men who were having sex with Dallas teenagers."

Hope had told me she didn't know the names of other men. Maybe she could identify other men from photos.

"What are you willing to offer for this information?"

"You claim that Hope was not in the same room when her friend fired the first shot Esposito. You also claim that Amber Davis asked Hope to get her involved with Esposito and his friends. If you convince us that is true, and your client gives us the names of Esposito's friends, we might be able to offer her a misdemeanor conviction with no more jail time."

"I would like for you to do something for me."

"What do you want?" Polk asked.

"I want you to take time to learn more about Amber Davis and Hope Riley. If you do, you'll quickly discover that Amber called the shots and Hope followed. In the meantime, I will discuss what you have asked with my client when she is released from jail."

While Polk never intimated anything, I took her offer to mean that Amber was not cooperating with the district attorney. I only wished that Hope had information she could give them.

CHAPTER 22

Hope

"Hope Riley," the guard called out.

"Yes," she replied, not knowing what would come next. A week earlier she had thought she would be released, but when it didn't happen, she had lost hope once again.

Hope had tried to be patient, but she had lost all faith when her lawyer told her she would have to stay in jail because of some problem with the ankle monitor.

"Your lawyer is here to take you home."

Hope's eyes brightened and she put on the face mask she had been given to wear anytime she was out of her cell. "They are releasing me?"

"Yes, but if I can give you some motherly advice, don't do anything that will make them send you back here before your trial.

No drugs, no alcohol, no relationships with adult men. With the virus, there is no telling when you will have your trial."

The guard took Hope's temperature, and it was normal. Neither the guard nor Hope realized she could be carrying COVID-19 and still have a normal temperature.

Hope had watched reports on the virus on the one television on the sixth floor during her stay, but she still didn't understand what it was. She had attended every class and every religious program made available to her until they had stopped giving the programs because of the virus. She hadn't expected to learn anything or become more faithful. She had participated just to have a way of passing the time.

For three months she had relived her modeling and bit part in the movie and her experiences with Henry Esposito. She had become convinced more than ever that he loved her and planned to eventually marry her. She longed for his tender touch, his encouraging words, and his thoughtful gifts, but that was all in the past. What could she do to replace that warm feeling when she was free?

Hope also thought about the cash she had stashed away in a hiding place no one, including her mother, would find.

She knew her classmates were on their spring break. Would her school allow her to come back on Monday? She hoped to see friends who had written to her while she was in jail and thank them for being kind.

Hope walked through the lobby to a counter where a guard in a mask gave her the clothes, cell phone, and other items she'd had with her when she was arrested. The only things she cared about were her cell phone, which she discovered could not be turned on until she recharged it, and her designer sunglasses, which she put on.

Hope looked at herself in a mirror and decided her first stop, after retrieving her money, would be the beauty salon that had streaked her hair and made Mr. Esposito say she looked like a movie star. Even though he wouldn't be there to compliment her, she was certain the boys in her high school would stare at her and the girls would be envious.

She thought about whether she would try and find another man who would pay her and wondered how the pandemic had affected hooking up with men for sex.

Hope thought about Amber. Would she be able to see her? Could they talk about the story they intended to tell? Did she even remember the story they intended to tell? Was life in the juvenile detention center as boring as her life had been in the jail? They had a great deal to talk about if she would be able to see Amber.

Then Hope saw her lawyer. She started to run up and give her a hug, but Ms. Sanchez put up her hand to stop her. Hope suddenly realized that might be unhealthy in the new normal Coronavirus world.

On their way to the car, a group of reporters asked questions. Gabriela responded to several questions and instructed Hope to not respond.

As she got into the passenger seat, Hope said, "Ms. Sanchez, thank you for getting me out of here."

"I'm happy we were able to make that happen. They say the country will be closed down for three weeks, so hopefully we can get your trial set sometime soon."

"Why is the country shutting down for three weeks and what does that even mean?"

"As Coronavirus infections increase, there is fear that our hospitals will be overwhelmed with patients and there won't be enough beds for the patients. You know something about math. Apparently one person can infect a dozen and each of those infected can infect a dozen. Pretty soon there are millions and millions infected. The medical experts claim that people must stay six feet apart. They call it social distancing. The shutdown means that only essential businesses can remain open, and people have been ordered to stay at home."

"You mean I won't be able to go back to school on Monday?"

"I don't think your school will reopen on Monday. It may not be open for the rest of the school year."

Gabriela looked over at Hope, who was fidgeting in her seat and changed the subject.

"I'm sure your mother will be happy to see you."

Hope smiled. "Yes, and I will be happy to see her and sleep in my own bed." Then she frowned again, remembering that her mother had been laid off.

"Is my mother okay?" Hope asked.

Gabriela was uncertain how to answer. She was sure Emma Riley was struggling financially.

"Your mom told me she will be okay when she has you at home with her."

"Will I be able to see Amber?"

"No, just as no one, including your lawyer, could see you in jail, no one can visit Amber."

"Can I have a video conference with her?"

"Maybe. Why do you want to talk to her?"

"We are best friends. We haven't talked to each other since we were arrested. I haven't been able to talk to any of my friends."

"I believe the assistant district attorney asked Amber to identify Esposito's friends with whom she had sex, and I believe she refused to identify them."

"What makes you think Amber refused?"

"Because the assistant district attorney asked me if you would be willing to identify the men," Gabriela responded. "She said if you identified the men, she would be willing to drop the charges and let you plead guilty to a misdemeanor. That is a great deal for you."

"I only saw other men at parties. I never had sex with any of them. I don't know any of their names."

"Would you recognize any of them if the police showed you photos?"

"Maybe, but I won't do that."

"Why?"

"I believe if I identified any of the men, me and my family would be in danger."

"What makes you think you would be in danger?"

"They are powerful men. They have families. They could hurt me, or my mother."

Gabriela parked in front of Hope's apartment complex.

"Do you want me to walk you to the door and make sure your mama is home?" Gabriela asked.

"No. I'll be fine."

"Don't visit any of Esposito's friends. Remember, stay at home. Even if you need groceries, let your mother get them. If you leave home during the stay-at-home order, they will revoke your bail. Can I count on you?"

"Yes." She touched her face, a gesture I interpreted to mean she would not stay at home."

"Did Henry Esposito know the police contacted you?"

"I don't know. He asked me and I lied, but I believe he knew I was lying."

"You knew that Esposito was having sex with other girls, right?" I asked.

"Yes, I knew."

"Then it's hard for me to understand what made you think you weren't a victim."

"He never forced me to do anything. I made the choices. I may be seventeen, but I am capable of making those choices."

"One last thing. Did you and Amber delete what was on Esposito's computer and wipe it clean after Amber shot him?"

Hope had a dazed look on her face.

"No, neither of us would know how to permanently delete videos and photos Mr. Esposito saved on his computer."

"Did anyone enter Esposito's apartment before Amber and you left in Esposito's BMW?"

"No."

"Is there anything else you want to know?" Hope asked.

"No but I want you to stay home, watch TV, spend time with your mother. Do not say anything about your case to anyone, especially Amber. You can't count on her to be your friend. Do you understand?"

"Why do I have to stay home? I saw on TV that it is okay to leave home."

"That is true in some places, but not in Dallas County. Stay at home."

Hope had watched TV every day in jail and the one thing she learned was that teenagers like her were less likely to catch the virus, and if they caught it, they were less likely to have complications. She had no intention of staying home.

Hope walked to the front door of her apartment. Trying to unlock the door, she dropped her keys twice before the door opened and her mom threw her arms around her. Both couldn't stop crying.

Later, after her telephone charged, Hope tried to call the juvenile detention facility where Amber was being held. When she learned that juveniles in the facility could not accept calls from friends, she asked the guard to let Amber know she had called.

Then, Hope started calling her other friends and planned to sneak out of the apartment to meet them.

When she and Amber talked by telephone the next day, Hope didn't realize that their conversation was being taped.

CHAPTER 23

Gabriela

When I got home that night, I had a thought for the first time. This pandemic could likely destroy my chance to run for Congress back home.

I woke up early the next morning and drank coffee. After my outside run and short weight training with the few dumbbells I had at home, I sat down at my computer and sipped my coffee. I opened the *Dallas Morning News* on my iPad. There on the front page I saw my color photo with Hope leaving the Dallas County Jail. The headline read: "Charged with Murder, Teen Who Didn't Pull Trigger Free on Bail."

I began reading the article.

> *Hope Riley, a gifted seventeen-year-old student at the Dallas Performing and Visual Arts High School was released from the Dallas County Jail on Monday*

after Judge Amy Foster reduced her bail and sufficient donations were received on a 'Free Hope' Go Fund Me page to post the bond for bail.

Ms. Riley, who turned seventeen the day her sixteen-year-old friend fatally shot and killed Dallas financier Henry Esposito, had been in the Dallas County Jail since January. She has been charged with murder, grand theft, and sex trafficking. Her trial had been scheduled for March thirteenth but has been postponed until May eleventh.

Robin Polk, the Dallas Deputy District Attorney assigned to prosecute the case, told the news that the two girls' real motive in killing Esposito was to steal his car and flee to Miami.

I found it interesting that during the stay-at-home order, this reporter had been allowed to go to the Dallas County Jail. That clearly wasn't an essential activity.

Judge Foster originally set Riley's bail at one million dollars, but after her trial was postponed indefinitely by COVID, the judge reduced her bail to one hundred thousand dollars.

The Dallas Morning News has learned that prior to his death, Henry Esposito was under police investigation for molesting teenage girls. A teen's mother notified the police after finding one-hundred-dollar bills in her daughter's purse and confronting her daughter. Police say the teenager later recanted her story and that is why they discontinued their investigation of Esposito.

On their way out of the jail, the News asked Gabriela Sanchez, Ms. Riley's lawyer, for a comment, and she said because of a court order she could not comment. Previously, Ms. Sanchez has asserted that her client is a victim of sexual abuse at the hands of Henry Esposito. He lured her into his web by helping her with modeling engagements and a small role in a movie made in Dallas.

Sanchez also reminded reporters that Dallas is second to only Las Vegas in the number of teenage girls trafficked and that sex trafficking does not always involve kidnapping or pimps.

"Just look at Jeffrey Epstein," she had said before Judge Amy Foster issued a gag order denying Ms. Sanchez the opportunity to communicate with the press.

Last August, thirteen girls were recovered and identified in Dallas as part of a nationwide operation called "Operation Independence Day."

The News asked Hope Riley what it had been like to be locked up as the only seventeen-year-old girl on the sixth floor at the jail. Ms. Riley declined to reply. "Hope was a bright and gifted girl attending the Dallas High School for Performing and Visual Arts with a future that included college, acting and modeling," her mother said.

Hope Riley's case highlights many problems with Texas law. In all but six states, including Texas, Ms. Riley would have been treated as a juvenile and not as an adult. Unlike thirty other states, Texas doesn't have a state statute that protects a sex-trafficking victim from facing charges on a crime committed while they were being trafficked.

"Traffickers like Henry Esposito are brilliant at finding young, vulnerable girls and finding how they can manipulate them," said UT Arlington professor Alice Andrews. "In this case, Esposito knew Hope Riley did not have a father and he judged her

high school talent show and knew she wanted to pursue an acting and singing career."

Hope was a victim. I just hope she realizes it before her trial.

I looked at the byline on the article and saw the writer was Olivia Davis. I wanted to contact her and at least thank her for pointing out that Hope was a victim, not a murderer.

Before I could call, my cell phone buzzed, and I saw the area code was 310, which I thought might be Los Angeles. I almost didn't answer, but at the last minute I did, and I heard the voice of the celebrity Rhonda Parker, who had helped young girls across the country. I had asked for her help to create a defense fund for Hope.

Parker had started defense funds for several victims of sexual abuse who had been charged with crimes. I hoped she would do the same for Hope and get other celebrities to participate.

"Is Hope a girl of color?" Parker asked.

"No," I replied. "What difference does that make?"

"Black and Hispanic girls are far more likely to be victims of traffickers. Was your client forced or coerced to have sex with the man she allegedly killed?"

"No. But, he groomed her, so he didn't need to force or coerce her."

"The Trafficking Victims Protection Act, passed in two thousand, defined a sex-trafficking victim as any adult involved in a commercial sex act that was induced by force, fraud, or coercion or in which the person induced has not yet reached the age of eighteen. Your client wasn't induced by force, fraud, or coercion."

"Neither were Jeffrey Epstein's victims."

"But none of his victims shot him. We have thrown our support behind minority girls who were trafficked by men. Your client is White. She is privileged. She doesn't need our help."

I couldn't believe what I was hearing.

"Hope's mother is single. She works two jobs to support her children. Hope is White, but she is not privileged."

"She is privileged. You are a high-priced lawyer, and you are representing her."

I knew I couldn't win the argument, so I gave up. Instead, I wished her well and called Father Michael to relate the news. He told me a parishioner had taken up Hope's cause and had continued the Twitter buzz with the hashtag #FreeHope that I had created and thousands of her followers had retweeted. She expected the #FreeHope social media posts to go viral over the next few days.

Father Michael directed me to a webpage that was titled: "Justice for Hope Riley," with her color photo taken while singing right after the title.

In the first paragraph, Hope is described as a seventeen-year-old White girl accused of capital murder, grand theft, human trafficking, and contributing to the exploitation of a minor. In the next paragraph, the webpage described Hope being approached by Henry Esposito after he judged a talent show contest at her high school.

Henry Esposito took advantage of a high school junior whose future could not have looked brighter. Join us now by contributing to Hope's defense.

I wondered how the webpage creator knew that fact, but I read on:

Her sixteen-year-old friend killed Esposito while he was engaged in sexual activities with Hope and her. Hope was there but did not shoot Esposito.

The website included a video interview of Emma Riley, who described her daughter as a devout Catholic with Christian values who had changed after she participated in her high school talent show last year. I wanted to know why neither Emma Riley nor Father Michael had bothered to share with me they were creating a video for a Free Hope website.

At the end, readers were asked to contribute and to sign a petition to free Hope Riley.

The last thing Father Michael said was because of the public outcry, I should be able to persuade the judge to dismiss the case. I protested that I had already filed a motion to dismiss, and Judge Foster had ruled against me. I was reminded of the PR firm that had interfered in my defense of Sparks Duval. The last thing I needed now was for my priest to tell me how to defend Hope.

I took note of one thing Father Michael had not said during our conversation. He never said any of the money that had been raised would be used to pay me. I knew that would be the first thing I would hear from Jack Wainwright and my partners who had voted against me taking Hope's case. Thankfully, we were still working from home so I wouldn't have to face them.

That night, Hope's case was one of the leading news stories on each of the Dallas local news stations. One of the stations had an exclusive interview with Emma Riley, who cried while answering the reporter's questions.

As I watched the news reports, in spite of not knowing what Father Michael and Emma Riley were doing, I was elated that Hope was getting national attention. I was convinced the national outcry would cause the Dallas District Attorney to drop the charges.

I was wrong. Even with all the publicity and petition drives, Hope Riley was still facing a murder charge, and no one knew when the Dallas courts would resume holding trials. When I agreed to defend Hope, I never dreamed a pandemic would delay her trial indefinitely. There was no turning back now.

I thought the trial delays were the worst thing to happen. But then people who had never met her took to social media to condemn Hope and condemn me for defending her:

Do the crime...Do the time

She's no victim. She knew what she was doing when she and her friend killed Henry Esposito.

The privileged White slut and her lawyer should be locked up and the key thrown away.

She took his money and then took his life and then escaped in his car. She belongs in prison.

Think of Henry Esposito's children. Because of Hope they will never see their father again.

Protest in front of Gabriela Sanchez's townhome to make sure she knows we know where she lives.

I decided I needed to make two phone calls. I called Father Michael first.

"Father, I'm not sure the media campaign is working."

"Why?" he asked. "What makes you think it is not working."

"The campaign is irritating Judge Foster and the district attorney. I had hoped he would drop the charges, but so far he hasn't."

"It's been successful. We've raised a ton of money for her defense."

"My law firm has asked me why the firm hasn't received any of this money you have raised."

"Because every penny is needed for the Free Hope campaign."

"Which you never sought my input for."

"We purposely didn't discuss it with you because Judge Foster issued an order directing you not to discuss the case with any of the media. I believe you told me it was a gag order. We believed it was best for you to be able to honestly say you knew nothing of the media campaign going on to Free Hope. Wouldn't you agree?"

There was no arguing with the priest. He was right about one thing: Judge Foster would have been livid if she thought I was directing the media campaign behind the scenes.

I decided our conversation wasn't getting anywhere and our law firm would never see any of the money that had been donated, so I wished Father Michael well and hung up.

CHAPTER 24

Amber

Amber Davis had been taken by surprise in mid-March when a guard told her that her friend Hope was on the phone and wanted to speak with her. *How could Hope call?* Amber wondered. When Hope told her that she was at home after being bailed out of jail, Amber didn't understand why. How could Hope be at home and she remained stuck in the juvenile detention facility?

They talked a few minutes about their experiences in jail. Amber shared that she had been taking classes in the juvenile facility until March 12th. Then, everything changed, and she had been going stir crazy ever since.

Amber described that since March 12, she had spent nearly twenty-four hours a day in the small room by herself, getting out only to shower or use the bathroom. They had shut down her classes and her counselor couldn't see her.

Her brother, Tyler, could no longer visit her, so her only contact with Tyler was during phone calls limited to ten minutes, and they sometimes cut off before ending. She ate meals in her cell and her only interaction was with the guards.

A week earlier a guard had handed Amber a tablet and showed her how she could access online classes. She had tried but she had given up out of boredom.

Recognizing they only had ten minutes, Hope passed on describing what she had experienced and went right to the point of her call.

"We need to tell the same story on what happened. You know I am your most loyal friend and I want to make sure I never say anything that would hurt you."

"Yes, I know you are loyal and would never hurt me," Amber replied, not disclosing that her attorney had told her that she must testify against Hope in her trial.

"I don't think anyone will believe we shot Mr. Esposito in self-defense. We need a better story," Hope said.

"I agree. What is our story?"

"Mr. Esposito gave you his gun."

"Yes."

"You didn't know the gun was loaded, right?" Hope asked.

"Right," Amber agreed, thankful Hope could not see her facial expression.

"And you panicked after the first shot."

"That is what I plan to say."

"And we took Mr. Esposito's car because we didn't think anyone would believe us."

"That is true," Amber replied.

"So, we no longer will say you shot in self-defense. Instead, we both will say the shooting was an accident, and we took the car because we were afraid. Right?"

"Yes."

"Your birthday is April eleventh, right?" Hope asked.

"Yes," Amber replied.

"Will they let your brother come to visit you?"

"No. It will be the first time we have not been together to celebrate my birthday or his."

"I know you must miss him."

Amber started crying out loud. She was both sad and angry and didn't know how to cope with her new reality.

No one really cares about how I feel.

With that, the girls wished each other well and said goodbye.

Two weeks after their call, Amber still didn't understand what was going on with the virus, but the adults who worked in the detention center seemed increasingly worried about catching it, and several of her new friends who had been accused of lesser crimes had been released. The staff wore masks and shields over their faces and had given each juvenile a mask to wear. Each day, a staff member came by and took her temperature. So far it had been normal, but the staff member told Amber that five teenagers and two staff members had elevated temperatures, had tested positive, and had been sent to the hospital. Amber thought staying in a hospital would be a far better option than being stuck in her tiny quarters.

When she spoke to Mr. Rizzo, he told Amber that he and other Texas lawyers were trying to get all juveniles released from juvenile detention so they could avoid getting the virus. He told her the lawsuit said the conditions inside the detention center were dangerous and unconstitutional because youths, like Amber, were at risk for exposure and were being held in their rooms for all but thirty minutes a day—and that the juvenile facility was not equipped to protect the teenagers from the virus. Amber finally understood for the first time why she was stuck in her room by herself and had no contact with the other teenagers and why each day a staff person asked if she was having suicidal thoughts.

The truth was she had those thoughts, but not because she planned to commit suicide. Rather, she thought the staff might send her to the hospital. When Amber replied she had suicidal thoughts, instead of sending her to the hospital, the staff increased the time they watched her.

When he met with her, Mr. Rizzo had told Amber that the district attorney was willing to offer her a deal if she would give up the names of the men with whom she had sex. He advised her that would not be a good idea because he was sure those men had lots of money; they could either give it to her and help free her mother or they could use to make her life a living hell. Amber had already feared what might happen to her if she gave up names, but she had no idea what the men considered to be lots of money they could give her.

Mr. Rizzo had also told Amber that the district attorney would be willing to offer a deal if she testified against Hope. Amber at first had balked at the idea. Hope was her best friend, and on occasion her lover. But as her time being isolated in her tiny quarters went on, Amber had begun to reconsider the offer.

What did they want me to say? she asked herself. Everyone knew Amber had pulled the trigger. Did they want her to say Hope was the mastermind and had told her to do it? If so, would she be willing to lie about her best friend to save her own skin?

Being by herself for almost all of every day gave Amber time to think, to question, and to search for ways to get out of the juvenile detention facility. She had read and reread each book a staff member brought to her. When that staff member stopped bringing her books, Amber had asked another staff member why and had learned the staff member had died from the virus. For the first time, Amber trembled from fear. Did the staff member give the virus to her? Was she going to die? She couldn't sleep. She couldn't concentrate on the new book she had been given. Fear overtook her and she lay in bed and cried most of the night.

April-May 2020

Chapter 25

Gabriela

I was preparing for Hope's trial when I received the call.

"Ms. Sanchez, I'm sad to report that your client is back in jail."

WTF "Why?" I asked.

"She was out with her friends in violation of the county judge's stay-at-home order, and she must not have realized that even with no ankle monitor, the police were keeping track of where she was. When Dallas police approached her, she tried to run."

"The police put her back in jail for violating the stay-at-home order? That makes no sense."

"Ms. Sanchez, I'm just telling you what happened. She violated the stay-at-home order, and given her exposure to COVID in the jail, she put others, including her friends at risk for catching the virus."

"Thank you for letting me know."

"Oh, and one more thing you should know."

"What's that?

"She spoke to Amber Davis by telephone and apparently neither girl knew their conversation was being recorded. They talked about getting their stories straight."

"What stories did they discuss getting straight?"

"They said no one would believe Amber shot Esposito in self-defense so their story now is that neither girl knew the gun was loaded when Amber pulled the trigger."

"That could be the true story."

"If it were true, they wouldn't have to get their stories straight."

She's right. Damn, damn, damn. Why didn't she follow my instructions? She is stuck in jail now until her trial, and with the courthouse closed, only God knows when that will be.

Hope was back in jail, and I was still working from home. At first, I had dressed each morning as if I was going to the office. By

April I rarely got out of my workout clothes while sitting in front of my computer. I continued working in workout clothes during May.

In the rare cases I was required to meet with someone on camera, I put on a blouse and jacket with my running shorts and running shoes below. I thought I must look awful since I hadn't been able to get my hair cut.

I missed being at home with my family. It had been fine when I could choose when to visit. Now, because of COVID, I couldn't visit them in person. Speaking to my parents and brothers and sisters and their children on FaceTime and calling my mother every day was not the same as visiting them in person. If only I had not agreed to represent Hope, I would be back in the Rio Grande Valley running for Congress.

I missed having a relationship. I hadn't seen Daniel for over a month. But it didn't cure me of wanting to get a hug. I hadn't even touched another person since the night I last ate dinner with Daniel.

After a few weeks, I had to visit four different stores before I could find one with toilet paper. There was no toilet paper or facial tissue on the shelves at the first three stores I visited. I also found no meat on the shelves of all four of the stores, in part because some of the meat packing plants had shut down and in part because, like toilet paper, shoppers were hoarding meat when it was available. I read articles saying there was a worldwide food shortage. At the time, there were signs that the spread of the disease was slowing, and that gave me some hope.

That hope vanished when I received the phone call from my father saying my grandmother had COVID, was in the hospital and was not doing well.

Chapter 26

Gabriela

I packed quickly and started driving to the Valley that night. On the way, my father called again to report that my grandmother had passed away while I was driving. I took an exit off I-35 and pulled into a gas station and started crying.

After gaining my composure, I continued driving home. When I arrived, I parked in front of our house and my mother and father came outside to say hello about twenty feet away from me. That was as close as we could be given the social-distancing directives. We all cried.

I called Lucia and told her I planned to stay in the Valley for Nana's funeral, only I discovered that because of the lockdown, we could not have a funeral. It would be delayed indefinitely. The funeral director suggested we have a Zoom funeral. I hated that idea and thankfully my parents did also.

I was allowed to visit her room at the assisted living facility and pick out the dress and jewelry she would wear in the casket. While in her room, I discovered dozens of letters I had written to Nana going all the way back to when I was in college. I asked the funeral director if I could put the letters in her coffin and he agreed.

I drove back to Dallas the next day, sobbing in my car. My life had changed dramatically in one month. I had lost my grandmother and more. Since I had been a little girl, I'd always had goals, a plan to achieve them, actions, and a way to hold myself accountable. Now I was stuck alone in my home with nothing to do and nothing to motivate me, my mind stuck on my grandmother, who I would never see again, and my family, who were an eight-hour drive away from me.

For the next nine days I joined my family's prayer time over Zoom. I was getting more depressed each time we met over Zoom.

Being introverted, I had always done well being alone, but like visiting my family, I was able to choose whether to be out with people or be alone. Having no choice was different. For the first time, I agreed with my mother who frequently told me I needed to find a husband. If I had one at least there would be two of us stuck at home.

I had thought I understood what it was like for Hope to be alone in a cell on the sixth floor of the Dallas County Jail, but I now realized, from my own isolation, that I had had no clue. I was suffering myself.

Chapter 27

Gabriela

While I had never visited a doctor, I have a mild case of obsessive-compulsive disorder. In my self-diagnosis, I counted always having difficulty dealing with uncertainty. I had never encountered uncertainty to compare with COVID-19.

When I go to sleep, I always place the opening to the pillow on the left side. When I dress, I always put my left shoe on before my right. At the golf course I always warm up with the same golf clubs, hitting each club the same number of times.

I started having weird dreams, or at least I thought they were weird. In one dream I could not remember where my classes were on the University of Texas campus. Worse yet, I couldn't remember my schedule.

In another dream, I was playing the lead in a play, only right before I was to go on stage, I couldn't remember my lines. My mind had gone blank.

In perhaps my worst dream, I was in trial and as I stepped to the podium to deliver a closing argument, I could not remember what I had prepared to say.

I did some research and was taken aback by what I found. Supposedly my dreams meant I was unable to deal with the world situation and that I felt helpless. If anything, finding out what my dreams meant increased my anxiety.

I certainly was anxious. I kept thinking of the worst-case scenario, fearing for my father and mother. They were at the age that was most likely to die from the virus, and my father was diabetic, which also increased his chances of dying.

Every time New York Governor Cuomo or President Trump came on television I turned them off. I didn't want to hear about how bad things had become or what was being done to curb the spread of the virus.

Before the pandemic, I could easily go all day without speaking to anyone. I could go months without drinking alcohol or taking my prescription for Xanax to overcome stress. After about a month of isolation, I was lonely, bored, and depressed. I lived for my work, and since all the courts were closed, I didn't really have any work to do. When I was busy working, I had lots of energy. Without work to keep me busy, I felt like a limp mop. I was burning out from being shut out of all human contact and not having enough work to occupy my mind.

Before the pandemic, I enjoyed coming home and recuperating by myself over a weekend. But now, for the first time, I craved having another person to share my bed and I wished I was married or at least had a live-in partner.

One day, while running outside, I was listening to iTunes music from the seventies. A few songs had played, then I heard the opening lyrics to a song. I had not heard the sone before, but when I got home, I searched for the lyrics and found:

> This is for all the lonely people
> Thinking that life has passed them by
> Don't give up until you drink from the silver cup
> And ride that highway in the sky
>
> This is for all the single people
> Thinking that love has left them dry
> Don't give up until you drink from the silver cup
> You never know until you try

I cried again. I was one of the lonely people thinking that life and love had passed me by and left me dry. I didn't want anyone to know I was depressed because they would see I was not the happy, successful lawyer they had seen in public.

It had been an incredibly hard couple of months. The one thing that kept me going was I had greater appreciation for my family, who had encouraged me to be successful and had comforted me any time I failed. Zoom calls with my family became highlights of my day.

I started drinking wine and lemon-drop martinis. Even though churches weren't allowed to hold in-person services, liquor stores were open. So wine, vodka, and limoncello were easy to come by.

At first, I stopped after one glass. By April, I was drinking two glasses of wine after drinking a martini every day. By May, I was consuming the whole bottle, after drinking two martinis, and I was starting earlier in the day.

Unable to sleep, I took Xanax each night to calm my nerves.

I told myself it was time to stop. In fact, I told myself it was time to stop several times. My father had been an alcoholic when I was growing up, and a doctor had told me I likely inherited it from him. After rehab, when I was in law school, he had been sober. Unlike him, I thought I could control my drinking, but as each day went by, I discovered I couldn't. I blamed my problem on COVID.

Damn COVID!

Chapter 28

Gabriela

Near the end of April, the governor had announced the first phase of the plan to open Texas. In the report, he noted the rapid increase of COVID-19 cases in nursing homes. The governor announced criteria for opening retail stores, restaurants, and other businesses at twenty-five percent capacity, but many businesses remained shut down.

In early May, a Dallas hair salon owner made the national news. It turned out she had continued offering services despite the state's order closing all hair salons. I would have represented her for free if she in return had cut and styled my hair. A judge sentenced the salon owner to a week in jail and fined her seven thousand dollars after the salon owner refused to comply with a cease-and-desist order, tearing it up on national television.

I thought that only in America, and only during a once-in-a-lifetime pandemic that had shut down the country would a hair salon owner become a national hero. At least one good thing had come out of her fifteen minutes of fame. Within a week, the governor had reopened hair salons and barber shops. I felt fortunate to have secured an appointment, and the next day, I sat in the chair with my mask in place. I gave my favorite stylist a fifty-dollar tip, knowing she had been unable to work for at least two months. As a single mother, she was so grateful to be back working again she started crying and fell into my arms.

I was lonely and wanted to interact with people. I tried a Zoom happy hour and met a guy who seemed nice. We started texting and before I knew it, he wanted to come over for what I described would be a one-night stand. I had many questions, including who he had been in contact with, if he wore a mask, if he had been in any big groups, if he had been tested…

A friend told me men and women seeking partners were posting on Craigslist in the activities section. I went online, and to my surprise, I discovered she was right. I clicked on a few of the posts. One man posted he wanted a woman to come over and shelter in place with him until it was safe to go back to bars. I quickly decided that was a terrible way to find male company during COVID.

Another friend told me about a dating app she was using. I was skeptical until she told me a woman had started it and that the women using the app had to make the first move. She said that gave her the opportunity to screen her potential dates in advance.

I asked if she was concerned about getting COVID from meeting with strangers. She claimed she required any men she met to show her they had tested negative and that she generally went to their house or apartment rather than a restaurant.

I thought I could try it and at least not be inundated with unwanted messages—or however the person made the first contact. I created a profile, uploaded a photo, and started looking. I found many potential candidates.

After two weeks of fantasizing, I contacted Sam Moody, a forty-year-old man who I could tell worked out regularly. He was also a lawyer, but because he was a corporate lawyer, I had never met him before. He responded to my contact, and after consulting with my friend on what to do, I gave Sam my telephone number.

He called and we set up a meeting at a coffee shop for the next morning. Even though it was a little chilly, we sat outside drinking coffee and talking.

As my friend advised, I told Sam I wasn't looking for sex. He smiled. When I asked why he was smiling, he told me that every woman he had met on the site had said they weren't looking for sex and none of them had meant it. That made me even more determined to not have sex with Sam.

At first, I thought I might be overanalyzing the situation. It would be the first time I'd had sex in a couple of months. I finally gave in and became one more of those women who said they weren't looking for sex and didn't mean it. We went back to my condo and within five minutes we were in my bedroom.

We parted an hour later, and I decided I would never contact him again. But I kept my profile on the dating site and looked for the next good-looking man.

Then, a couple of days later, a package was left on my front porch. I opened the package and found three Sandalwood Rose candles and a handwritten note: "Thinking of you. Sam."

To say the least I was surprised. Men had given me flowers before, but no one had ever given me candles. When I lit the candle that night, I loved the smell. If there was such a thing as a romantic smell, the candle Sam sent had it.

I called Sam to thank him, and we agreed to meet again for dinner the next night.

I wanted to get my mind off having sex, but I was bored. To change my focus, for the first time, I played golf on weekdays. Prior to the virus I had only played golf on weekdays for charity events. In

April and continuing in May, I played golf as many as five times a week.

Some of my partners found it even more difficult to work from home. Their kids were at home and were doing their best to attend their classes virtually. My partners had many distractions with which to contend while trying to stay productive. Some told me their internet did not have enough bandwidth to support their children being online for school at the same time they were online for work.

Whenever I started feeling sorry for myself, I thought of Hope. Except for the three days when she was out on bail, Hope had been stuck in the Dallas County Jail in virtual isolation since January. She was essentially in solitary confinement twenty-three hours a day and facing the possibility of catching the virus in the infested jail.

I couldn't do anything to help her. I couldn't meet with her in person. I couldn't meet with the prosecutor to persuade her to make a deal. Even if I could meet with the prosecutor, she would have no incentive to make a deal, since Hope could not give her the names of other men. Even though Judge Foster had reset the trial date to May, we both knew as we approached May, that the date was in jeopardy.

I was right. On May 4th, the Texas Supreme Court suspended all jury trials until further notice. Judge Foster issued an order canceling Hope's trial and advising the district attorney and me she could not reset the trial until the Texas Supreme Court established a date for the restarting of jury trials. In March, I had thought things would be back to normal and courts would be operating in person by May. When Judge Foster didn't even set a revised trial date, I finally admitted I had no idea when jurors would be back live in Dallas courtrooms.

I couldn't do my job because of the virus. My hands were tied. I couldn't convince a jury to find her not guilty because the court was not open and there were no juries to be seated. I read that after the latest order, the Dallas District Attorney predicted there would be no jury trials until at least September, if not beyond that date.

Given what had happened so far, I had no reason to believe Hope's trial would take place until there was a vaccine, and God knows when that would be. My thought was confirmed when the Texas Supreme Court issued an order extending the date for no jury trials to September.

I worried about Hope's mental health, in part because I worried about my own mental health. When I called Hope, I could hear her gasp and then heard her seemingly unable to catch her breath. She was having a panic attack, but other than telling her to take deep breaths and stay calm, I felt helpless.

Working with Lucia remotely was challenging, but we had so little work to do that it was no longer crucial that we be in the same place. We both tried to maintain the routine we had established at the office. For example, we started work at our normal time with a Zoom meeting to go over what we planned to do that day. My office phone calls were transferred to my cell phone. Lucia and I ended each workday as we did at the office by going over what we wanted to accomplish the next day. We kept up with our routine during March, but by April we abandoned the morning and afternoon Zoom meetings and only conversed when we had something to go over together.

The only cases I could pursue were two contract arbitration cases. I normally assigned contract arbitration cases to younger lawyers, but I had agreed to take them on simply to keep from going stir crazy at home. The arbitrations were held on Zoom with three arbitrators, the witnesses, and the lawyers on camera.

One day in May while sitting at home, my cell phone buzzed. I saw the area code was 959. I had no idea where the 959 area code was and I debated whether to answer, thinking it might be a robocall. I finally answered.

"Ms. Sanchez?" I heard the voice say.

"Yes," I replied.

"This is William Scott."

I knew I had heard that name, but I wasn't sure where I had heard it. "Mr. Scott, I don't believe I know you.

"You don't. I write true-crime books. You may have read one or more or at least become familiar with my books."

Bingo, that was where I had heard of William Scott. He had written a true-crime book about a Texas murder case with which I was vaguely familiar.

"I haven't read any of your books, but I am familiar with them," I replied. "What can I do for you?"

"I want to write a book about your client's case, and I want to work with you before and during the trial."

A true-crime writer who wanted to write a book about Hope's trial in my mind meant he was convinced she had committed the crime. I thought he would be working against me, not for me and Hope.

CHAPTER 29

Gabriela

"Why do you want to write about Hope's case?"

"Because I believe she is innocent."

"I believe she's innocent also, but I am under a gag order to not speak to the media about her case."

"At this point I don't need for you to tell me about your defense."

"Then why are you calling?"

"Because I can act as your unpaid investigator if you are willing to work exclusively with me when the trial is over."

"And what would you investigate for me?"

"Don't you want to know why Amber had the gun in her possession and why she pulled the trigger?"

"Hope told me she doesn't remember what happened until she heard the first shot. Amber told Hope afterward that she accidently pulled the trigger."

"Doesn't it seem odd to you that Esposito would give Amber a loaded pistol?"

"Not really, I understand Esposito took photos and shot video of Amber, Hope, and other girls with guns and knives."

"I doubt the gun was ever loaded. Have you seen the photos and videos?"

"No, the police haven't shown the photos and videos to me."

"What if Amber wanted to shoot Esposito?" Scott asked.

"The district attorney believes Hope and Amber purposely killed Esposito, and they created inconsistent stories about what happened."

"What if you can show that Amber is a compulsive liar. Wouldn't that help your defense?"

"Sure," I replied. "But how will I prove that to a jury?"

"Well, to write my book I will be investigating Amber's past. Aren't you also curious why Vincent Rizzo took over representing Amber?"

"I figure one or more of the men who don't want Amber to name them paid Rizzo and Amber decided he would do a better job than Junior Jones," I said.

"Those men had a motive to get rid of Esposito. He knew about their sexual misdeeds with teenage girls and those men could not risk his talking if the police arrested him. I will try to determine which man or men hired Rizzo and what, if anything, they are giving Amber not to identify him or them."

"Mr. Scott, one more thing for you to investigate. Amber Davis kept a journal. If you are able to get ahold of it, we might learn more about whether she pulled the trigger for a reason."

"I will talk to Amber's foster home mother and see if she will give me a copy of her journal. I already know she was an escort on Backpage before she approached Hope. She jumped at the chance to make more money from Esposito's wealthy friends."

I couldn't hire a private investigator to help me. Jack Wainwright had put the kibosh on that when I brought it up. Scott had a reputation for finding evidence in a case that everyone else missed. I could use Scott's help to come up with Hope's best defense, so I told Scott to go ahead and investigate.

Afterward, I turned to my original thought. I discovered that Scott had never written a book about a defendant who the jury found not guilty. His readers bought his books because at the end the police found the killer and the jury convicted him. Was that his intent in Hope's case? Was Scott telling me he believed Hope was innocent while scheming to find evidence proving she was guilty? I ordered each of his books to find out if he could be trusted.

June 2020

Chapter 30

Gabriela

Day after day I became more bored and more disillusioned about what was happening. Hope was still stuck in a cell on the sixth floor of the Dallas County Jail, Joe Biden had become the Democrats' nominee for president, and after a Minneapolis policeman choked George Floyd to death on May 26, people started rioting in the streets, night after night, even in Dallas.

In Dallas the police used chemical deterrents and rubber bullets to disperse crowds. On June 1, Dallas made the national news when the police detained hundreds of protestors on the Margaret Hunt Hill Bridge, and that started the sharp criticism of the Dallas police chief.

Maybe our country was at the beginning of a revolution. Our cities would have protests that led to riots night after night. But each night if I watched the news, I learned what happened in Portland the night before. Each Monday, I saw a report on how many people were shot and how many people were murdered on the streets of Chicago.

I had been raised by two Democrat voters. I had voted for each Democrat who had run for president, but in 2020, for the life of me I couldn't figure out how my party, with more than twenty other candidates running against him, had settled on a man who, if elected, would be the oldest person to take the oath of office as president.

My father reminded me that President Kennedy had been forty-three the day he took the oath of office, and he took over from President Eisenhower, who was seventy and the oldest man to have held the office up until that time. In his inauguration speech, Kennedy had said that the torch had been passed to a new generation of Americans.

I was disappointed that the torch would not be passed to a new generation of Americans. Instead, Biden and Trump were both older than Bill Clinton and George Bush. How could that be?

My father told me people in the Rio Grande Valley weren't supporting Biden like they had supported every Democratic candidate before him. I understood that while I couldn't support Trump, I was disappointed the Democrats had selected Biden. It made me wish even more that I could run for Congress in 2020. But it was too late now.

One day I paused and looked into my closet and for the first time I realized that since March 12th, I had not worn three-quarters of the clothes and shoes I saw, including skirts, dresses, and heels. I had no reason to wear any of those clothes while staying at home, or running outside, or playing golf.

By the middle of June, I had quit watching any news stations. To avoid the news, in the evening, I binge watched *Boston Legal* and *Ally McBeal*.

The COVID cases were once again rising in Dallas and in Texas. My law office remained closed and I continued to work from home, but the state allowed bars to reopen only they couldn't serve at the bar, only tables that were six feet apart. The Dallas superintendent of schools said he believed there was a seventy-five percent chance Dallas schools would be open for students in August. I don't normally gamble, but I would have bet against schools being open in August.

On one Saturday in June, I agreed to hand out food at Lonestar Park. It was a long, tiring day standing in the hot sun with my mask and gloves on, but I later learned we had handed out food to over seven thousand cars that day, making it all worthwhile.

When I agreed to defend Hope in January, I never dreamed she would remain isolated in jail in May, then June, with the likely possibility she would be stuck in jail for months to come. While some hearings could be handled by Zoom, I couldn't defend Hope and confront any witnesses testifying against her in a Zoom hearing.

One day in late June, while I was walking Bella and listening to an audiobook, the narrator paused, and my phone rang. I looked at the caller ID and saw it was Jack Wainwright. Knowing he was not calling to offer any good news or wishes, I thought about letting the call go to voicemail. Instead, I answered.

"Gabriela?"

"Yes."

"Jack Wainwright, I'm calling with some bad news to share with you."

He had confirmed my initial thoughts.

"As you know, the firm's revenue is drastically down, especially in the litigation practice group. We must take some drastic measures to reduce our costs. We have to let some of our staff and young attorneys go. Since the case you are working on is not generating any revenue for the firm, we must let Lucia go."

I gasped out load. My stomach tightened and blood rushed to my head. I wanted to lash out at him, but I knew he would take that as a sign of weakness.

Wainwright continued.

"I want you to call Ms. Lozano and let her know."

"By early next year, litigation will be at a peak," I finally replied, slurring my words. "The courts will be so backed up that for the following months—and maybe years—the litigation practice will be booming, and that's even before considering all the COVID-19 related cases. Once we let our most talented people go, we may never get them back."

"Have you been drinking?" Wainwright asked.

"No," I lied. "I just finished working out and I'm trying to catch my breath."

"Then take a moment and catch your breath."

"Okay," I replied, being more careful.

"There are many talented people out there," Wainwright continued. "If we can't get Ms. Lozano back, we'll find another assistant for you."

"Jack, I believed you when you announced to all of us that the firm put its clients first, its young lawyers and staff second and its partners third. I never thought our partners were so greedy that we would abandon our staff when they need us the most. You must have trouble sleeping at night."

Wainwright didn't respond for several seconds. Finally, he said, "I'm not going to argue with you. Just do what I asked."

So, this is his payback.

July 2020

Chapter 31

Gabriela

Wainwright had accomplished what he had set out to do when I told him I planned to defend Hope Riley. I could either leave the firm and have Lucia work for me or I could stay in the firm and be forced to tell my loyal assistant she had lost her job.

Wainwright had one other ace up his sleeve. If I left the firm, he could delay the repayment of my five hundred thousand capital contribution for three years. That put me in an even more untenable position, I would have no income coming in for months until there was a vaccine and courtrooms were back open for trials. I had saved money over the years, but I wasn't sure if I had enough if I left the firm because I wasn't sure when clients would start paying me again.

I considered calling Christopher Duval. I knew he would gladly hire Lucia, but he would expect something from me in return.

When I was about to give up, I came up with an idea and called Leo Baretti. I had successfully defended the famed trial lawyer's daughter, Gina, when she had been indicted for refusing to testify in a grand jury bribery investigation of her client and the governor. Leo had told me if I ever needed anything, I could call on him.

After three rings, he answered his cell phone.

"Leo, Gabriela Sanchez." I had always wanted to call him Mr. Baretti, but he had insisted I call him Leo. I was still uncomfortable saying Leo.

"Gabriela, how nice to hear your voice. I hope you are okay."

"Thank you, sir. I'm fine, but I have a favor to ask of you." I told him Wainwright had laid off Lucia to get back at me for taking on the defense of a seventeen-year-old girl whose mother couldn't afford to pay us.

"I've read articles about your client and I've seen many social media posts supporting her and some awful and mean posts about her."

"She and her mother can't pay us, and because of the Coronavirus her trial has been postponed indefinitely."

"What can I do to help you defend her?" Baretti asked.

"I probably could use your help since I have never defended a case in Dallas County court, but what I need for now is for your firm to hire Lucia. I will reimburse you for what you pay her so she can help me," I said.

"It's not necessary for you to reimburse us. I'd like for you to join our firm."

I had never thought of joining Baretti's law firm.

"Leo, that is very kind of you, but my firm has made leaving the firm difficult financially."

"I understand, but I hope you will consider joining us. I know Gina would appreciate having you as a partner."

Leo Baretti was a great trial lawyer known for his ability to read what witnesses, judges and juries were thinking, but I was sure he had misread what Gina would think having me as her partner. Two alpha females in the same firm would not likely work out well.

"I'll call Lucia and tell her that your firm will hire her," I said.

"Let her know we are all working from home and I will have our office manager contact her to fill out the paperwork."

"Yes, sir."

"Stay safe, Gabriela."

I was staying safe from the virus, but being alone was leading me to drinking more alcohol.

August-September 2020

Chapter 32

Gabriela

June and July saw a rise of COVID-19 cases in Dallas. The Dallas County judge attributed the rise in cases, in part, to gatherings over Memorial Day weekend and the Fourth of July as well as protests on the streets of Dallas in response to the George Floyd choking death.

After telling Lucia of our new arrangement, I went back to doing research, hoping to find Hope's best defense. I started reading every book written about Jeffrey Epstein and watched every television show produced. I learned a great deal on how he allegedly recruited young girls, kept them coming back for more, and persuaded them to recruit their friends.

I watched a Netflix series based on a scandal at an elite Italian high school. That series focused on high school girls who engaged in prostitution as a way to get money and access to goods they could not afford.

While the Netflix series was informative, none of the high school girls were poor and none of them had shot any of the men who paid to have sex with them.

In August, Emma Riley was on television urging people to get behind the "Free Hope" movement. She asked for donations, asked people to sign petitions, and she even took out newspaper ads chiding the Dallas District Attorney.

I called Robin Polk and told her that she should dismiss the charges against Hope.

She scoffed at the idea.

"Your client's mother has enlisted the aid of Hollywood personalities to use social media on your client's behalf. That has only made our resolve greater to get justice for Henry Esposito's children."

I could tell the media campaign was starting to make Polk, and likely her boss, uncomfortable. With that in mind, I explained that Henry Esposito had been a father figure for Hope. He had helped her get a small role in a movie and helped her move forward with her modeling career. She had no motive to kill him. If anything, she had a motive to keep him alive and keep her relationship with him.

"Isn't that something for the jury to decide?" Polk asked.

"It shouldn't have to wait for a jury. Hope is rotting away in the Dallas County Jail. She is suffering mentally and physically. You should drop the charges now."

"We will prove that Hope and Amber planned to murder Esposito and take money and his car to Miami. If Hope had no motive to murder Esposito, why would she watch her friend shoot him and leave the scene?"

"Robin, the girls panicked." I chose to not argue that Hope wasn't even in the room when Amber fired the first shot. "They left the scene out of fear no one would believe the shooting was accidental. You've made my point. Like I said, Hope had a motive for Esposito to stay alive and continue to help her. Hope lost a great deal when he died."

There was silence at the other end. Finally, Polk said, "I believe I can make a deal for your client to plead to manslaughter and serve ten years. What you must realize is that with all the public fervor your client's mother has created, there is no way we can dismiss the charges now."

"Ten years! Hope's life will be ruined."

"Then you should get prepared for the fight of your life. I will win this case and your client could face up to fifty years."

"What can we do in the meantime?" I asked. "Hope's health is deteriorating each day she is stuck in isolation in jail."

"She shouldn't have violated her bond."

"I agree and I told Hope to stay at home, but I don't think you appreciate what is happening. Hope's locked up twenty-three hours a day. She eats her meals by her toilet. She can't talk to her mother and she has no contact with anyone other than the guards. Hope's lost a lot of weight, her hair is falling out, and she thinks she will get COVID any day."

"I'm sorry, but I am not willing to let her out again. COVID is getting worse, not better, and she could potentially infect someone. If the guards believe her health is in jeopardy, they'll send her to a doctor."

I hung up and called Father Michael. After some small talk about when church services would be live again, I got to the point of my call.

"Father, you and Mrs. Riley have created a media firestorm that has pushed the district attorney's office into an untenable position. They can't drop the charges now. They need to take some of the money you have raised and hire an investigator to help me with Hope's defense."

"Why? What kind of investigator?"

"One best known for helping defendants who can find out why Amber pulled the trigger and shot Esposito."

"I know you are trying to help Hope. Isn't it your job to figure out why Amber pulled the trigger?"

"The district attorney claims she and Amber planned and murdered Henry Esposito to take money and his car and escape to Miami. That is the theory I am up against.

"Hope claims she was not a victim and that Esposito did not take advantage of her. She will not be a good witness in her own defense. We need to learn more about Amber."

"Who do we hire? I don't know where to look for the best investigator."

"I'll find the best and get back to you."

"Okay. One other thing I need to tell you."

I gasped. *Here we go again.*

"Do you know Andrea Kessler?" Father Michael asked.

"Sure, I know her. She's the nurse who retired last year."

"In June, Andrea volunteered to go back to work at the hospital to help with the surge in patients," Father Michael said. "She somehow got the virus earlier this month and died in the hospital two weeks later."

"That is so sad. I know her family is devastated."

"Indeed. I wanted you to know that the virus is deadly."

"Father, I'm so sorry. But as you once told me, sometimes bad things happen to good people and we can't do anything about it. This could be one of those times. Let her family know they are in our prayers."

***

Later that month, I read that more Texans had died from the Coronavirus in July than any month. That was after we had been told that the virus would be less of a problem during the summer.

I have always been an optimistic person, but like many people, I'd lost my optimism in 2020. Being inundated with news about disease, death, and loss of jobs was taking an emotional toll on me.

I sometimes thought I was having a bad dream and when I woke up, I'd be able to go out to eat at my favorite restaurants, travel anywhere in the world, shop at the small stores, and visit my family.

I felt wiped out. I had no energy. The one thing that kept me going was the burning desire to persuade a jury that Hope Riley was innocent. I did a Zoom call with Hope each day to give her as much hope about her future as I could muster.

One day during our call, I asked, "Did Henry Esposito try to separate you from your mother?"

"What do you mean?" Hope asked.

"Did he try to control you and pull you away from your mother?"

"No, Mr. Esposito tried to take the burden from my mother. He paid for my voice lessons, my acting lessons, and for my modeling portfolio. He told me he wanted to help me so my mother wouldn't have to sacrifice so much for me."

"Did he ask you anything about a traumatic event in your life?"

"He asked me about how I felt to not have a father in my life. I don't understand why you are asking me these questions."

I was exploring whether he had brainwashed her. At that point I wasn't sure if it made any difference, but I wanted to know.

"I am trying to understand as much as possible about what he was trying to do in his relationship with you."

"He told me he wanted to help me achieve my dreams and that's how he acted toward me, and he did just what he said."

While "he deserved to die" was not supposed to be a defense to murder in Texas, if the jury saw Hope as a victim, they would at least think her molester was a bad guy. I had spent months going over in my mind how I could best defend a girl who did not think she had been Esposito's victim. Sadly, Hope still viewed Esposito as a saint.

October-November 2020

Chapter 33

Gabriela

"Gabriela, this is Congressman Moreno, I need your help."

"What kind of help?"

"I want you to come down to the RGV and campaign with me. Our people need to hear from someone who knows them and knows me."

I smiled when he said RGV, it's how locals refer to the Rio Grande Valley.

"Why do you need me?" I asked.

"Because I am running against a flamboyant Republican woman who has captured the attention of my constituents."

"How can that be?" I asked. "Your constituents love you and they haven't voted for a Republican in my lifetime."

"This election is different. I want you to come down and see. People are no longer just voting for the party of John Kennedy just because they are Catholic, and their parents and grandparents voted for Democrats. As you know, people here care about their family, jobs, and safe communities. Trump knows that and he is tapping into those concerns. There are caravans of people supporting Trump."

"Who is the candidate you are running against?"

"Roberta Reyes. She's running on a platform of pro-freedom, pro-life, pro-religion, and most importantly, pro-guns. Her campaign commercials tie me to Beto O'Rourke. She campaigns in jeans, boots, a cowboy hat, and a gun on her belt. She's even labeled me as a socialist who wants to defund the police. I am not anti-guns. I certainly don't want to defund the police. I don't support abortion on demand. And I have railed against the riots in the streets. Yet she is making those false claims in commercials."

"There's no way she can beat you. How is your campaign going?" I asked.

"My doctor has warned me I have many of the pre-existing conditions for COVID-19, so I have tried to reinvent the way I am campaigning. Zoom campaign events are not the same as meeting with people in person."

I thought about what the congressman had said. He was reinventing the way he campaigned because of COVID-19. Would I have to reinvent the way I try cases? When I defended Hope would jurors be in the same room? Would they be wearing masks? Would they be sitting isolated from each other and me by plexiglass shields? Would witnesses wear masks and sit behind plexiglass shields?

I had watched a few courtroom television shows that were filmed after the spread of COVID. In one show, the judge and jury were on a Zoom call. In another, the jury was in a different room or rooms. It was all bizarre and not how I wanted to defend Hope. I needed to see the witnesses and jurors faces live and in person. Zoom trials, like online schooling, would be a disaster.

"Congressman, are you really sure you want me to come down when your doctor is warning you about catching COVID?"

"Take a test before you come, and I will also. We'll stay at least six feet away from people and require everyone attending the rally to wear a mask."

"When do you want me to come down?" I asked."

"This Saturday, so we can do two to three rallies."

After we hung up, I searched Roberta Reyes on Google. She was indeed an interesting woman. In all of her photos she was wearing a sleeveless blouse, showing off her toned biceps, tight jeans with a gun strapped to her hip, high-heel boots, and designer sunglasses. Reyes was an attractive woman, and I could see why she appealed to at least the male voters.

In Reyes's YouTube ads, it was clear she was running as a major Trump supporter who brazenly fashioned herself as passionate patriot. In one of her ads, she played a video clip of Beto O'Rourke saying at a debate he planned to take guns away, after which she stood tall, holding an AK-47 on her hip.

I wasn't sure how having me campaign with him would help Congressman Moreno. I had agreed to come home to be with him in part because I would have the opportunity to spend time with my family.

On Saturday morning I met Congressman Moreno at Starbucks and we rode together to the first rally. When I got into the car for the first time, I noticed bags under his eyes and wrinkles on his forehead. He had aged just in the last few months. I understood why he had wanted to retire and come back home from Washington.

My job at each of the rallies was to introduce the congressman by telling my story on how he had helped me get a scholarship to Notre Dame law school and outline the many things he had done in Washington for the RGV. As he requested, I wore casual clothes and a University of Texas mask. It was one of many different ones I had purchased since March. It was a mask that went around my neck rather than over my ears, so when I spoke, I pulled the mask down to my neck. I admit I got a rush out of firing up the crowd for the congressman.

When he took the stage at the first rally, Moreno began by talking about his family, his family business, and the work he had done to improve the lives of the American people whose families had come to the Valley from Mexico and Central America. In Spanish, he said, we are "Estadounidenses de origen Mexicano"—we are Americans of Mexican descent. That line drew a thunderous applause. In closing, to my surprise, Moreno talked about my father and me and my promise to come back to the Rio Grande Valley to help our citizens.

He told the audience that he had asked me to run for his seat this time and I had agreed to run, but that was before COVID delayed my defense of a young seventeen-year-old girl who was the victim of a Dallas financier who had trafficked her. He said I unselfishly continued to defend the girl after COVID delayed her trial indefinitely, and that this led him to run in 2020—his last term. If they gave him their vote, he planned to pass the baton to me at the end of his term. He reached over and raised my hand.

I also understood why I wanted to return to the Rio Grande Valley. Congressman Moreno was a successful businessman who gave it up to serve the people. I was sure I wanted to give up my law practice to serve the people in the Valley.

When I looked at the local newspaper the next morning, Congressman Moreno and I were on the front page in a color photograph with a lengthy article about our rallies, including the congressman's statement that he wanted to pass the torch to me if reelected and his praise for my courage defending a seventeen-year-old trafficking victim. The article was picked up by both the Dallas and Fort Worth papers, so it was no surprise on Monday when I received a call from Judge Foster's office scheduling a Zoom hearing that afternoon on my violation of her gag order.

Robin Polk and I sat silently for five minutes before Judge Foster finally came on the line.

"I've called this hearing to remind Ms. Sanchez that I have issued a gag order. I do not want this case tried in the media, and it's become a media circus with the defendant's mother and priest trying to influence any jury members. Mrs. Riley posted a full-page ad in the Dallas newspaper telling the district attorney to drop the charges against her innocent girl. Ms. Sanchez, you must make this stop."

"Your Honor, I have tried to stop the publicity about the case, but I don't have any influence over what my client's mother says or does on the internet or news."

"Ms. Polk, what do you have to say about this?"

"Your Honor, I've told Ms. Sanchez that the campaign by the defendant's mother has put us in the position where we can't even offer her client a plea deal, much less dismiss charges. If we dismissed charges now the public would conclude that either we succumbed to pressure or we should not have charged her client with murder in the first place. Beyond that, I have nothing to say."

"Well Ms. Sanchez, because of the efforts being made on social media to prejudice jurors, I plan to set your client's trial for the first day they allow us to hold in-person trials. You will need to be ready quickly; your client's case for trial could be set with very short notice."

I was taken aback. I had no idea when Dallas County would start jury trials. If it turned out to be January, I would have only six weeks to prepare for trial, and I would have no help. I had wanted a trial date sooner rather than later, and now I had one with lots of work to be done to get ready, including persuading my client that she was Henry Esposito's victim, not the love of his life.

***

I had to persuade Hope during our Zoom meetings. In our first meeting, I started: "Hope, are you aware that Henry Esposito was having sex with other girls, including Amber?"

"Yes."

"But he wouldn't let you have sex with any other man. Didn't you think that was unusual?" I asked.

"No, he told me I was special, and he wanted me all to himself."

"Hope, I know Henry Esposito told you that you were special, but he was having sex with many girls, including your friends, sometimes more than once a day. He wasn't treating you like you were special. Can you consider the possibility that Henry Esposito was taking advantage of you?"

Hope became angry.

"Ms. Sanchez, several teenage boys have tried to have sex with me. Henry Esposito gave me voice lessons, acting lessons. He got me a part in a movie that was made in Dallas. He paid a photographer to create a modeling portfolio for me. He did all those things because he cared about me. He always asked permission before suggesting we have sex. Who do you think took advantage of me, the teen boys or Mr. Esposito?"

She had a point, but not one that helped her defense.

"Hope, I sense you are angry at me. My goal is to find your best defense to a murder charge that, if you are convicted, may result in you spending the rest of your life in prison. I respect what you believe."

Hope frowned, and I changed the subject.

I was stuck. I couldn't convince Hope that Henry Esposito had victimized her. She was in denial. I wanted to argue that Hope had no motive to murder the man who gave her so many opportunities. The only problem was she had five hundred thousand reasons for him to die.

November 2020

CHAPTER 34

Gabriela

On November second, I took the early flight down to visit my family and my grandmother's grave site for the Day of the Dead celebration. We celebrated her life on that day.

On the third, Congressman Moreno was reelected, but it was by the smallest margin in his career. I called to congratulate the congressman, and he told me that would be the last time he ran for office. He encouraged me to come back home and start preparing to run for his seat in 2022.

I was making great progress when I received a call from William Scott, the true-crime writer.

"I met with Amber's foster mother," he started.

"Did you see the journal?"

"No, her foster mother looked and couldn't find it in Amber's room. Maybe she destroyed it. You'll have to guess what she might have written in the journal."

"I need to figure out if Amber wrote anything the day of the murder."

"Amber's foster mother could only tell me that Amber said she was going with Hope to Henry Esposito's apartment to celebrate Hope's birthday. Her foster mother also said that Amber had told her that day that she and Hope would make a lot of money."

"Did she ask Amber how they would make lots of money?" I asked.

"Yes. But Amber just smiled and walked away."

"Amber's foster mother told me that Amber had confessed that she preferred girls to boys and that she wanted to spend her life with Hope," Scott reported.

"Did the foster mother say anything else important?"

"She said Amber was making a lot of money, and when she asked, Amber would not tell her how she earned the money."

"Her foster mother had to know it wasn't from working at McDonalds. Anything else?"

"I got the impression that Amber made well over one thousand a week and the foster mother made her share some of that."

"What made you get that impression?"

"She seemed upset that Amber had been arrested and I could tell it was not because of concern for her foster child."

"What did Amber do with the money?" I asked. "I don't believe she has a bank account."

"Good question. If she hid cash at her home, I'd bet the foster mother took it, But I don't know. I only know she had no motive to shoot Esposito. She was making lots of money having sex with Esposito and his pals."

"What if one of the men paid her a large sum of money to kill Esposito before he was arrested?"

There was a long pause, then Scott said, "Like you questioned before, where is the money if that happened?"

"What else can you tell me about Amber?"

"Her foster mother told me that Amber has lied many times about where she was when she was gone from the home and that she never told her she was prostituting herself to earn money for her new clothes."

"That makes sense," I said.

"Her brother told me that Amber did not want to become like her mother and end up in prison. It turns out that Amber has spent more time visiting her mother in prison than she has spent with her at home. Her brother told Amber that she was just like their mother. Even if that was true, he still hurt her feelings."

"Did her brother know anything about what Amber did with the money the men paid to her?"

"I asked and he said he had suspected Amber was prostituting herself, but he had no idea what Amber had done with the money."

"Amber's had a tough life," I remarked.

"For sure," Scott replied. "What she lacked most as a girl and teenager was a female role model and adviser to give her that motherly advice and guidance. Being in and out of foster homes, Amber never had someone make rules and discipline her when she broke them. I'm sharing all this with you because that background will influence how she testifies. In her eyes, there is no rule requiring her to tell the truth, the whole truth and nothing but the truth."

"I agree. That will make my cross-examination more difficult."

A question came to my mind at that moment.

"Do you believe Amber was on drugs the day she shot Esposito?" I asked. "If she was high, it might explain why she pulled the trigger three times."

"I don't know. I'll continue my investigation. If her attorney lets me talk to Amber, I will interview her."

I supposed I could subpoena the journal, but I hadn't decided whether that would be a good strategy.

In mid-November, I received more bad news. I read the latest Texas Supreme Court Emergency Order and found jury trials had been delayed until at least the first week in January. Once again, I had been as ready as I could be to defend Hope. I would have to start over again how many more times?

Damn. Will this case ever end?

November-December 2020

CHAPTER 35

Roberto Sanchez

Roberto felt his cell phone vibrate, and when he picked it up he saw Gabriela's name on the screen.

"Papá, should I come home for Thanksgiving? I am worried that if I come home, I might bring the virus with me and not even know it."

"What do you think?" Roberto asked.

"If I stay in Dallas, it would be the first time I haven't spent Thanksgiving weekend with you, Mama, and the family. The Dallas County judge is urging everyone to limit their Thanksgiving celebration to those in their immediate family."

"Maybe you should stay in Dallas."

"But Papá, I read that more people planned to fly over Thanksgiving weekend than any other time since the pandemic began in March. Let me speak with Mama."

Roberto put his wife on the phone and heard her urge Gabriela to come home. She told Gabriela that we would all enjoy our meal outside with spacing between each other.

Roberto came back on the phone.

"Gabriela, I recommend you get tested for COVID two days before your flight to make sure you don't have it. Call me to let me know the results."

A few days later, Gabriela called and told her father that the test came back negative. But she said she had spoken to a friend who told her the test she had taken was not as reliable as some of the others. She said she had become worried again.

Roberto suggested that she take a wipe on the flight and wipe down the tray and armrests. He also told his daughter to keep her mask on during the entire flight.

Shortly after the scheduled arrival time, Roberto saw his daughter exit the terminal with her roller bag. He put his daughter's suitcase in the trunk and held out his elbow to greet her. They both wore masks in the car on their way to the family house.

Gabriela seemed worried while in the car, so to alleviate her concerns, Roberto asked if she had any of the COVID symptoms. Gabriela replied that even though she felt fine, did not have a fever or shortness of breath, she was still worried she might somehow have COVID and not even know it.

As they drew closer to home, Roberto asked, "How is your case going?"

"Papá, I've never felt more pressure to win than this case."

"Even more than when you defended the billionaire?" Roberto asked.

"Far more," she replied. "While it was important and put pressure on me, Sparks Duval only had his reputation at stake. Hope has her whole life ahead of her at stake. I feel pressure like I have never felt before. I haven't had a full night's sleep for the last month."

"Have you been drinking over these last few months to take the pressure off?" Roberto knew the answer.

"Papá, I've been bored, stressed out, and lonely staying at home for the last several months. Occasionally drink a glass of wine or a lemon-drop martini."

Roberto thought his daughter was depressed and anxious. He had sensed that long before there was a pandemic.

"Gabriela, you never just occasionally drink a glass of wine, or a lemon-drop martini. You need to stop now before you get ready for the trial."

"I can stop at any time, Papá," she said. "I've done it before, and I can do it again."

Roberto Sanchez knew from his own personal experience it was not easy to stop drinking at any time.

"Focus on preparing to win. Lawyers who are afraid of losing generally didn't care enough for their client to be well prepared. I know you. You will care enough to be sober and well prepared, and the jurors will know you care."

For the first time since she got in his car, Roberto saw his daughter smile.

"Thank you," she replied, "I needed you to tell me that."

"Have you figured out the best way to defend Hope?" he asked.

"No, she refused to see herself as a victim, and with the trial scheduled for January fourth, I still believe her best defense is that Hope wasn't in the same room, didn't know that Amber would be given a gun and pull the trigger, and she had no motive to want Henry Esposito dead."

"I thought you said Esposito rewrote his will leaving her five hundred thousand. That's a motive."

"Hope claims she didn't know what he wrote in his will."

"Did her friend know what he had written in his will?"

"I don't know."

"Amber is going to lie. She will likely say Hope was with her and either told her, or gave her some signal, to pull the trigger. How are you going to show she is lying?"

"I've got some ideas. I've had to put them down on paper because the trial keeps getting postponed. I want to see how the jury reacts to her."

They continued talking and Roberto told Gabriela to focus on why Amber shot Esposito and who loaded the gun she used.

Gabriela had thought it was possible one of Esposito's pals who was afraid of being caught may have given her the idea of shooting him and fleeing the state.

Roberto smiled and shook his head. He wanted to remind his daughter that taking on a case for a client who could not pay was a mistake. He thought she had made a mistake even before the pandemic caused Hope's trial to be delayed over nine months.

"You've got only a few weeks to sort it out," Roberto said.

"My trip here will give me time to think about family. I need that, and when I get home, I will sort it out."

"Your mother is most anxious to see you. So are your nieces and nephews."

Thanksgiving dinner was different from any other. They ate outside on tables Roberto and his sons had set up with plywood between card tables. They were apart from each other and each wore a mask, except when they were eating. It was the first time Gabriela had eaten Thanksgiving dinner without her grandmother.

On Friday morning, Roberto took Gabriela back to the airport. On the way, he told her in no uncertain terms that she had to stop drinking alcohol now and focus on preparing Hope's defense. She asked if he would come to Dallas and help her with the trial, and he said he would if he had no other trials at that time.

As Gabriela got out of the passenger's side of the car, Roberto came over and embraced his daughter and whispered in her ear. Then he handed her a locket that had been her grandmother's.

"Nana wanted you to have this. Take care of yourself. Get Lucia to come work at your condo so you have the help you need close by."

He pulled his head back to make sure his daughter knew exactly what he had meant by his comment.

She was sobbing while staring at the locket. She nodded, turned, and walked toward the terminal.

The following Monday, Roberto received a call from his son, Roberto, Jr.

"Fernanda has COVID," he began.

"What?" Roberto asked.

"Yes, Fernanda apparently got COVID when she was out with her teenage friends and we tested positive also."

"Damn," Roberto said, thinking about whether Fernanda had gotten close to his mother-in-law or his daughter.

When their call ended, Roberto called his daughter. He went over his conversation with Roberto, Jr., and then asked, "How are you feeling?"

"I feel tired, but I think that is stress from preparing for the trial," she replied. "I haven't worked out since I got home because of feeling tired."

"I recommend you get tested again," Roberto said. "Feeling tired is one of the symptoms."

"I'll be okay, Papá."

"Your brother felt tired when he first had it also. Get tested."

"Papá, I read an article in the Dallas paper about jury trials resuming soon. That means Hope's case could start in early January, as scheduled. A Dallas judge has created a plan for in-person jury trials. Apparently, jurors and witnesses will wear see-through shields so their faces can be seen. How can I get ready for a trial in less than a month if I have COVID?"

"If you have COVID, ask the judge for a continuance. She certainly isn't going to want you in her courtroom if you can infect others. Don't just get one test. Even if a test is negative, get a test each week until the trial."

The next day, Gabriela called back and told Roberto that she hadn't been able to sleep because her sinuses were clogged.

Right then Roberto knew for sure—his daughter had COVID, and he knew that last thing she would want would be for COVID to delay her client's trial.

December 2020-January 2021

Chapter 36

Gabriela

On Tuesday, I woke up with aches and pains after a poor night's sleep. I continued doing research on my brainwashing theory until I started to get the chills. My sinus issues had gotten worse. I could not blow my nose nor breathe thru my nose. I could not get warm. But I didn't have a fever. Since I couldn't get any meaningful work done, I scheduled a test for the next day and went to sleep at six o'clock, something I had never done before.

I decided on the test I had been told was the most reliable, but I knew I wouldn't have the results for a couple of days. When I woke up the next morning on December seventeenth, I didn't have chills, which I thought was a good thing. They took my temperature at the test site and it was normal. I took it throughout the day, and it was normal, another good sign. I felt good other than a headache from my sinuses. I was dehydrated, and I could not breathe through my nose. I knew those were bad signs.

Over the next couple of days, I waited for the test results. In some ways I felt better and in some ways I felt worse. On Saturday, the nineteenth, I woke up after really good sleep and felt better. Again, I had no fever. I took my temperature every hour to make sure. My temperature was normal each time. For the first time on that Saturday, I lost my smell and taste. This was very troubling because I had not eaten anything in two days. At ten o'clock my phone rang, and I saw the call was from the testing facility. When I answered, a doctor was on the other line and he told me I had tested positive for COVID.

I had no idea if I would be able to defend Hope on the fourth of January. I called my father and told him I tested positive and would not be home for Christmas. As I said it, I realized it would be the first time I had not spent Christmas Day with my family. I rarely cry, but I cried to myself, hoping my father wouldn't hear me.

On Sunday, I woke up and felt better, but I still had no taste or smell and no energy. I had no other symptoms, and for that, I thought I was one of the lucky ones. I thought about whether being physically fit helped me.

On Monday, I woke up and had more energy. I was ready to do something other than just sit in my condo thinking about Hope's defense. I set up a Zoom call with Hope. When I told her that I had COVID, she lowered her head. When she raised it again, she was crying.

"Please tell me you will be okay before my trial."

"I don't know, Hope. I hope so, but I don't know," I replied. "I have a lot of work to prepare so I can give you the best defense."

What was I to do now? I knew if I told Judge Foster that I had COVID she might postpone the trial, and given the eleven-month backlog of cases, Hope would be stuck in the Dallas County Jail for months to come. On the other hand, if I didn't tell Judge Foster that I had COVID, I wasn't sure I would have the energy necessary to get ready and to go through a grueling trial.

I mulled over my choices for several minutes and I became more stressed thinking about it. Finally, I said hell with it, we're going to trial on the fourth of January. I did a Google search on how to get my energy back after COVID. I found a diet, exercise program, and drinking plenty of water to maintain hydration.

That night I didn't sleep well. I had another weird dream. In this dream it was January third and I had lost my files. I couldn't find what I needed for Hope's defense. I never found what I needed, but worse yet, when I was asked the next day to deliver my opening statement, I could not remember what I had planned to say, and everyone was looking at me as I was tongue-tied. I woke up in a cold sweat. I don't think it was from COVID. I think it was because of my fear of losing Hope's case.

As it turned out, having COVID didn't matter, I learned in late December that the courts remained closed, and Hope's trial was postponed once again.

I spent New Years' Eve at home and fell asleep before midnight. I had no desire to go out, and even though I was happy that 2020 had finally come to an end, I was still tired from COVID and didn't have enough energy to make it until midnight.

A few days later, I was walking on the treadmill when Lucia called me.

"Did you see what is happening?" she blurted out.

"Slow down. What are you all wound up about?"

"They've overrun the police and stormed the Capitol," Lucia said. "Trump's people are in the Capitol. It's a rampage."

I turned on my television and couldn't believe what I was seeing. It was stunning. Protestors were inside the Capitol. They had overrun the Capitol police trying to stop the electoral count. I saw Trump signs, Confederate flags, body armor, and helmets. They were striking the police with pipes and baseball bats. I thought I was in a third-world country.

I was glued to my television for the rest of the afternoon. Finally, it dawned on me—I could have easily been a member of

Congress forced to evacuate. Would the mob have come after me? What had our country become?

I continued preparing our defense over the next week. On January the fourteenth my heart sank again when I read the Texas Supreme Court issued the thirty-third Emergency Order, further suspending jury trials until April first. The administrator of the courts told a newspaper that even if Texas courts get back to normal by April, they will have a backlog of around 10,000 cases that would have been tried by a jury. That meant Hope's trial might be held long past April.

If the further delay wasn't enough, I was concerned that when it was finally time for the trial, those who would show up for jury duty would be predominantly White middle class or wealthy since the virus had disproportionately struck the poorer communities.

Would jurors be required to wear masks? Would jurors be seated six feet apart? Would witnesses wear masks? All of those unanswered questions created more concerns. I had never tried a case where I couldn't see the facial expressions of the witnesses and the jurors.

Each delay set Hope back further. I continued to be worried she would take her own life.

I called Robin Polk to ask if she would support my motion to release Hope on bond for a second time.

She laughed. "Why should we support your motion when staying in jail may cause your client to wise up and accept a plea."

"Robin, she is not going to plead to something she didn't do."

"Then I guess unless you can convince Judge Foster to release your client, she's going to be stuck in jail for at least a few more months."

I filed a motion to release Hope on bond that day. Two days later, Judge Foster convened a Zoom hearing on my motion. I looked on my computer screen and saw Hope, the judge, and Robin Polk.

After introductions, Judge Foster invited me to make my argument.

"Your Honor, I have asked that you release Hope Riley on bail again. As you know, other than the few days she was out on bail, Hope has been in the Dallas County Jail for over a year. During that time, she has essentially been in solitary confinement for up to twenty-three hours a day. She has lost a year of school. Both her physical and mental health have deteriorated dramatically. Studies have shown that isolation is a common risk for suicides of teenagers generally, especially during COVID, and even more so for teenagers isolated in jails. I am worried she will be one of those victims. She has written me notes saying, *I am going crazy in this place. I can't do it anymore.*"

I had one other motive for getting Hope out on bail. I wanted her to regain the look I saw when I first met her. I wanted Hope to gain back the weight she had lost, exercise, and get her hair done as I had first seen it. Studies show that attractive defendants are generally given more benefit of the doubt by jurors. Having spent a year in jail, Hope had lost the innocent, girl-next-door look I had first seen.

I continued. "Your Honor, Hope needs to see a mental health specialist. She's suicidal while rotting away in jail. Her guards have found suicide notes."

"Ms. Polk," Judge Foster said on the screen, "What does the district attorney have to say about this motion."

"Thank you, Your Honor. We oppose releasing the defendant on bail. She fled the state after committing the murder. She had her chance and blew it by not staying home during the pandemic. She could have easily infected people with whom she came in contact. We have her on suicide watch. The guards at the jail will make sure she is safe."

She paused, and I started speaking again. "Your Honor, what is happening in this country is appalling. You can read about how district attorneys are extracting unconscionable plea deals because defendants are stuck in jail with no trial date in sight. That is what is happening here. Ms. Polk has offered a plea deal that will ruin Hope Riley for life. She deserves better. Since she cannot get a speedy trial, she deserves to be released on bail."

Finally, Judge Foster spoke. "I had set the Hope Riley trial for March of last year. It has been postponed again and again. I've learned the Supreme Court has issued a new order delaying jury trials once again. This time until at least April. I most certainly understand why the defense does not want to conduct this trial over the internet. I have children who were stuck at home before schools reopened last fall. So, I understand first-hand what isolation has done to our children."

I thought a *but* was coming next and I was right.

"But as Ms. Polk said, the defendant in this case fled the state once and when she was out on bail, she couldn't follow the rules. With vaccinations taking place I believe her trial will be in April and I will see to it that she receives all the mental help we can give her in the meantime."

Hope's head dropped and I saw the tears streaming down her face.

"Your Honor. Just look at Hope and you can see she needs mental help immediately."

"Ms. Sanchez, I told you I would see to it she gets the help she needs."

When it was just the two of us on the Zoom call and Hope had regained her composure, she asked, "Why do you want me to see a therapist?"

I didn't tell her the whole truth, only a partial truth.

"You've gone through a lot being isolated in jail over the last year, and I believe a therapist can help you deal with that."

"Okay," she said and nodded.

I also wanted the therapist to deal with the fact that Esposito had groomed her and taken advantage of the fact that Hope had no father figure in her life. I also wanted to learn more about why she struggled to remember the first time Esposito had sex with her or what happened right before Amber shot him.

I wasn't convinced that Judge Foster would get Hope help, so I set up an appointment the following week for Hope to meet on a Zoom call with Dr. Jennifer Logan, a therapist and college professor who was also a potential expert witness on sexual exploitation of teenagers. With Hope's permission, I shared what she had told me with Dr. Logan.

After meeting with Hope, Dr. Logan called me. I asked Dr. Logan if she had any ideas about Hope's failure to remember what happened when Amber shot Henry Esposito.

"Are you familiar with EMDR?" Dr. Logan asked.

"No," I replied.

"EMDR stands for eye movement desensitization and reprocessing. It is used to help victims of traumatic events by helping them recall what happened. Through the therapy Hope may be able to recall what happened the day Henry Esposito first had sex with her, and the day Amber shot him."

While speaking to Dr. Logan, I did a search and found that in a case involving the sexual assault of a minor Texas appellate court had allowed testimony by an EMDR expert.

"I'm not sure it is a good idea for Hope to remember what happened the day Amber shot Henry Esposito," I said. I worried over what Hope might remember that might impact whether she could testify in her defense."

"I understand," Dr. Logan replied.

After giving it much thought, I asked Dr. Logan to meet with Hope and try the EMDR treatment.

Later I got some much-needed good news when my father called. He told me that he and my mother had just returned from the hospital, where each of them had received their first COVID vaccination and they were scheduled to return in three weeks to receive the second dose.

"Wow, Papá. That's good news. I think my reservation number for the vaccination is something like 75,000, and so far, less than 10,000 have received the first shot."

I told my father about EMDR and the treatment I planned to get for Hope that might help her remember what happened the day Amber shot Henry Esposito.

"Do you want her to remember what happened that day or is it better she doesn't' remember?" he asked.

"What if she remembers right in the middle of her cross-examination?" I asked. "I'd rather know in advance of the trial."

"Then let me know what she says happened."

It turned out that even the rapid eye movement therapy didn't help. Dr. Logan called after meeting with Hope and told me she thought Hope's memory loss was not a result of being traumatized.

"I think she was given a drug that makes the victim feel woozy and lose short-term memory. It usually does not come back. One such drug is something called Versed or Midazolam. This is most commonly used prior to a medical procedure. It can be given orally. I believe it is possible, or maybe even probable, that Henry Esposito gave this drug to Hope more than once and on the day he was shot."

That gave me an idea on how I might prove Hope wasn't aware of what was going on until she heard the first shot and things seemed to be brighter both at home and with Hope's case until I received a call from William Scott.

"I recently spoke with Darla Esposito. She has filed a suit today to contest her ex-husband's will, specifically the bequest of five hundred thousand dollars to your client. She claims your client is not entitled to the money because she murdered Esposito."

"What law firm is representing her?"

"Glenn Roberts. They are the same firm that represented her in her divorce case."

I wasn't surprised.

"That seems greedy of Darla given she received millions of dollars in insurance for their children and the bulk of Esposito's estate that had to be valued at well over one-hundred-million dollars."

"With Darla, it's not about the money," Scott continued. "And I don't think she mourns her ex-husband. It's her way of sticking it to a young girl she believes seduced her ex-husband."

After speaking with Scott, I called Hope and told her about Darla's will contest. I was surprised by her response.

"I don't care. I don't want the money. Let her have it."

I had a feeling Emma Riley might have a different take on defending the lawsuit.

"May I let your mother and Father Michael know about the suit and what you've told me?"

"Yes," Hope replied. "As long as you tell her I don't want the money."

February-May 2021

CHAPTER 37

Gabriela

In early February, I read that weather forecasters were predicting record cold temperatures and snow in the Dallas-Fort Worth Metroplex. I didn't have a winter coat or the kind of boots to get around in the cold and snowy weather. I went to the mall and purchased what I thought I needed. I assumed the condo association would plow my driveway, so I wasn't one of the Dallas residents who went to Home Depot or Lowe's looking for a snow shovel.

On February fifth during the night, I could hear the freezing rain. I woke up the next morning and saw the ice on my driveway and street and decided to work again from home and not run outside. Later that morning, my cell phone buzzed with an alert about a major car crash in Fort Worth. I turned on the news and could not believe what I was seeing. By that time, over six people had been killed and 130 cars and trucks had crashed.

As the day went on, I saw more videos of what had occurred, including a tractor-trailer truck that had crushed cars and even sent one flying in the air. I could hear people screaming in one of the videos. I hadn't considered leaving my condo that day, but now I was too stunned to get any meaningful work done.

Over Valentine's weekend, record cold temperatures came to Dallas, along with a snowstorm. Then all of a sudden it was cold in my condo as I had no power. I read on my iPad before the battery ran out that the electrical company had planned rolling blackouts, but they had lasted longer than planned in my area of Dallas and it would be days before power was restored in some areas.

I had opened my faucet in the kitchen and shower, but on Sunday I had no running water, and ice still covered the roads. I thought I should move into a hotel so I could at least take a shower. I called the Smiths and postponed our meeting until Friday and stayed at home.

On Tuesday, my pipes burst, and I had no one to help me deal with the mess in my condo. My dog, Bella, was terrified. I didn't want to call Daniel, so I called Christopher. He and a couple of his workers came to help me clean up the mess.

"You can come stay with me," Christopher said.

I didn't know what to do, and Christopher must have noticed.

"You don't need to worry about me. You'll have all the privacy you want."

"Can I bring Bella with me?" I asked. "She's well trained."

"Sure," Christopher answered.

I packed a suitcase and put it in the back seat of Christopher's car, along with Bella, some of her toys, and her bed. Thirty minutes later, I was lying comatose in his guest bedroom with Bella across my stomach. I had never been so exhausted, even when I had COVID. That night, I dreamed of hearing what I would have to pay out of pocket to restore my condo.

I reluctantly agreed, expecting to be out of pocket several thousand dollars. Even though my heart wasn't in the case, it was worth taking an hour or two to meet with the Smiths in return for not worrying about the cost to restore my condo.

Christopher surprised me. He was a true gentleman, and he spent several days helping me clean up the mess at my condo. I don't know what I would have done without his help and support. One afternoon, after hours of work together, I gave Christopher a hug. He held me tight. It was my first contact with a man in months, and for the first time since COVID, I felt someone cared about me.

A few days later, the temperature was in the forties, I had power back, so I came back to my condo. Now I was waiting for a plumber. They were working eighteen hours a day and still couldn't keep up with the demand.

I called my insurance company and started searching for restoration companies. My condo was a mess, and I could only imagine what it would take to get it repaired. It took a couple of weeks before an expert came to my condo. After going over the mess, he told me the walls, hardwood floors, and all of my kitchen cabinets would all have to be replaced, and he said I had to leave the condo for a couple of months for all that work to be accomplished.

Where was I to go for two months, most likely before, during, and after Hope's trial? I went back to the Valley and worked out of my father's office while the plumbers and the restoration company did their work. I discovered that it was hard to get workmen to my house, and when they were available it was hard to get the materials they needed to do the work. I was just one of thousands who needed restoration. So any time I received an estimate of time to get something done, I learned to double it.

Finally, after three months, the workmen finished restoring my home and I could get back to a somewhat normal home life.

On May fifteenth, the headline in the local section of the Dallas newspaper got my attention. It read:

Jury trials to resume in Dallas County on June 1 with hundreds of backlogged cases.

That day I received a call from Judge Foster's administrator telling me that Hope's trial would be the first in the judge's courtroom and it would begin on June first.

Finally!

June 2021

CHAPTER 38

Gabriela

I couldn't sleep. My mind had been racing, and I could feel my heart beating.

I had never done well waiting for an event. In golf, the leaders tee off last. When I was young, I dreaded being in the final twosome. It meant I would have hours from the time I woke up to arriving at the first tee. I preferred to get up and go out and get right to it. In golf tournaments, I was playing to win for myself. In trials, I am advocating for another person. The pressure I felt defending Hope was far greater than any other case I had tried. Her future life depended on me persuading a jury that she was innocent. She would either be able to finish high school, go to college, and pursue her life and career dreams or she would be stuck behind bars in a Texas state prison for most of the rest of her life.

I had waited for well over a year to defend Hope. Her original trial date had been in March of 2020 and now it was June of 2021. I had started and paused my trial preparation four or more times over the thirteen months. Each delay added to my anxiety about the case.

I'd tried dozens of cases, but I still had trouble sleeping the night before a trial started and each night during the trial. I felt the pressure and had recurring self-doubt.

I tried the case in my head. I could see the courtroom and the jurors, and I visualized giving the jury my opening statement, cross-examining a witness, and making my final argument. In my dream, the other side always does something that takes me by surprise and throws me off my plan. It's usually something I have overlooked, meaning it is on me. That Sunday night before the start of Hope's trial was no exception, I might have gotten only a couple of hours of sleep.

Even though no celebrities had gone to bat for Hope, Emma Riley's #freeHope campaign had ignited a national following. Hope's plight was featured on cable news, opinion pieces in newspapers far from Dallas and almost daily online. My every move in court would be scrutinized each night by so-called legal experts on each of the news networks. Robin Polk's every move would be scrutinized by the Dallas minority community. If Hope was found not guilty, no one could predict what might happen in the streets of Dallas.

I prayed. I promised God that if he would give me the right mindset, strength, courage, and the persuasive skills to convince the jury to find Hope not guilty, I would never ask for his help in another trial.

I knew I was well prepared. I had decided the case turned on whether the jury believed Amber's story or Hope's story. I knew Amber would stick to her story, so I was focused on how I could show the jury that Amber was lying.

Early on Monday morning, my cell phone rang. I saw it was William Scott, the true-crime writer who had been following the case.

"Miss Sanchez, I have a gamebreaker for you," Scott started with an excitement in his voice.

"Yes?"

"I have interviewed teens in the juvenile facility where Amber Davis has been staying. Olivia Turner is one I interviewed. She can testify that Amber Davis told her she purposely shot Henry Esposito so he could no longer be between she and Hope. It wasn't an accident and Hope had nothing to do with the shooting."

I had to get to court right away, so I told him I would call him as soon as Hope's trial finished that day, although I knew my mind would be on this new information all day.

Later, I arrived at the courthouse with the new COVID protocols. There was plexiglass everywhere. They took each person's temperature when entering the courthouse. 180 potential jurors were seated socially distanced in the central jury room, all wearing face shields so we could see their faces.

I had told Father Michael and Emma Riley to pack the courtroom with mothers from our Parish. I wanted jurors, Robin Polk, and Judge Foster to know that the community was watching and what side they were on. Sadly, I learned that no spectators would be allowed in the courtroom.

We spent that morning selecting jurors. I had hired a jury consultant and she was seated next to me. She had told me earlier that we did not want to have Hispanic or Asian women on the jury. When I asked why, she explained that Asian and Hispanic women were not likely view Hope as a victim. She thought African American and Caucasian women would be a better selection.

We both agreed that it was likely some of the potential jurors had been molested during their teen years by an adult. But if we asked that direct question during our questioning of jurors, that would lead to embarrassment at best and resentment at worst. We decided to phrase the question in broader scope. Even though "he deserved to die" is not a defense in Texas, I wanted to select those jurors who believed Henry Esposito deserved to die.

Eventually, twelve jurors and two alternates were seated a few feet apart from each other in the gallery of the Dallas County courtroom. Our tables were flipped so instead of facing Judge Foster, we faced the jurors in the gallery. I saw the chair where witnesses would sit on a stand next to the jury box. I noted that when I wanted to make an objection, I would have to turn around to communicate the objection to Judge Foster.

A man was behind a camera on a tripod in the back of the courtroom live-streaming our trial for anyone who wanted to watch. I felt like Hope's trial was an experiment in new court COVID protection procedures.

I heard Judge Foster speak from behind me. "Ms. Polk, you may make your opening statement to the jury now."

After introducing herself and explaining she was the attorney for the county of Dallas in this case, Robin Polk spent no time getting to the heart of the prosecution's case.

"Ladies and Gentlemen, this case is relatively simple. You won't need to figure out who shot Henry Esposito. The defendant and her friend Amber Davis shot and killed Mr. Esposito. Amber Davis will testify that the defendant gestured for her to pull the trigger and shoot Henry Esposito. After they shot and killed him, the defendant and Amber Davis took his money, stole his BMW, and took off from the scene heading toward Miami. They were tracked down and caught while driving in Baton Rouge, Louisiana, where the defendant made a video-recorded confession. It is really that simple.

"But it all started two years before when the defendant seduced Henry Esposito after he judged a talent contest at her high school. She took advantage of Mr. Esposito. She used her charm to persuade Mr. Esposito to pay for voice lessons, acting lessons, a photographer to create a model's portfolio. She even convinced him to help her get a small role in a movie made here in Dallas.

"You will learn that prior to the defendant seducing him, Henry Esposito had been a loving husband and father to his two children. He had contributed to many causes that you likely know of and see here in Dallas. Everything changed that day when he judged the talent contest and met the defendant.

"You will learn that the defendant had a good reason to want Henry Esposito to die. In fact, she had five hundred thousand good reasons. Some day before he was shot, Mr. Esposito had written a new will including a provision giving the defendant five hundred thousand dollars. She and her friend signed the handwritten will as witnesses. That was the motive that drove the defendant to suggest that her friend pull the trigger.

"The defendant may claim the shooting was an accident, but that could not be further from the truth. After the defendant and her friend shot Henry Esposito, they took five thousand dollars, stole his

BMW car, drove home, cleaned up, packed their bags, and started driving for Miami.

"While her friend Amber may not have known the gun was loaded, the defendant intended to murder Henry Esposito. They were under the impression that no one would find them in Miami, and if they were found, Texas would not extradite them back here because they had shot and killed a man who was a predator. Some people in Texas believe there is a defense titled 'He deserved to die.' That is not true. After you hear all the evidence, we ask that you deliberate and find the defendant guilty of murder in the first degree."

Robin Polk paused as if to let her words sink in, turned, and walked back to her table and sat down.

I looked up at Judge Foster, who said, "Ms. Sanchez, you may make your opening statement to the jury."

"Ladies and gentlemen, my name is Gabriela Sanchez. I represent Hope Riley." I opened my palm toward Hope. "She is the girl who on her seventeenth birthday went with her friend, Amber Davis, to see the man who had been trafficking her for sex since she was just fifteen. Hope is a victim, not a criminal.

"Ms. Polk told you that this case is relatively simple, and you won't have to figure out who shot Henry Esposito. Do you remember that?

"On that point we can agree. This case is relatively simple, and you won't have to figure out who shot Henry Esposito. Hope Riley did not—I repeat, did not—shoot Henry Esposito. Amber Davis shot Henry Esposito."

I paused to make sure each juror was listening. "Ladies and gentlemen, Hope Riley wasn't even in the room when Amber Davis pulled the trigger the first time. After she heard the shot, she ran into the bedroom, screamed, and reached for the gun. Amber Davis fired two more times."

I had just made a commitment to call Hope Riley to testify in her defense. She was the only one who could say where she was when Amber fired the first time.

"After shooting him three times, it was Amber who took Henry Esposito's money from his wallet. It was Amber who decided they should take Henry Esposito's BMW and head for Miami. Hope wanted to stay here and tell the police what had happened."

I still had no clue what was in Miami and why Amber wanted the two of them to go there. I had originally theorized that one of Esposito's friends might have hired Amber to shoot Esposito and then to get her out of the way he had deposited money in a Miami bank. I had investigated and found nothing to support my theory.

"You will learn that while on the road, Hope called her mother, who encouraged Hope to come home and tell the police what happened. Hope wanted to come home and Amber kept on driving. For some reason, Amber wanted to drive to Miami."

I told the jury that Hope didn't know that Esposito had left money for her in his will. Hope had no motive to kill Esposito. To the contrary, Hope's dreams of a modeling and acting career were pinned to the opportunities Esposito was giving her.

"So, ladies and gentlemen, you will hear that Henry Esposito paid teenage girls, including Hope, to have sex with him, He started sexually exploiting Hope when she was only fifteen years old. He groomed her and was a brilliant manipulator for whom Hope would do anything. He sexually abused Hope at the same time he gave her expensive gifts, took her on trips in his private jet, and provided opportunities for her to advance her future career in return for Hope having sex with him whenever he desired. Hope's future depended on Henry Esposito. She wanted and needed his continued support. He purposely created Hope's dependency on him. His behavior was shocking.

"Henry Esposito was not just satisfied abusing Hope Riley. He wanted to sexually abuse her friends as well, including Amber Davis.

"The evidence will show that the police were investigating Henry Esposito. They could have arrested him, but they didn't.

"Instead, Esposito was free to invite Hope and Amber Davis to his apartment on Hope's seventeenth birthday. After celebrating

Hope's birthday, Esposito had Amber and her pose for videos and photos. A little later he had them pose with one of his guns. Amber held the gun and pulled the trigger the first time and nothing happened. Then she pulled it three more times and killed Esposito while Hope was in shock and reaching for the gun.

"When you hear all the evidence," I turned and pointed my open hand once again at Hope, "I am confident you will find that Hope Riley is innocent."

I turned and walked back to the table and took my seat. I thought Judge Foster might take a break, but instead I heard her say, "Ms. Polk, you can call your first witness."

CHAPTER 39

Gabriela

As I expected. Robin Polk called Darla Esposito as her first witness.

Darla's job was to come across as the grieving widow, place blame on Hope for stealing her husband, and humanize Henry Esposito. I expected to hear how he had been a wonderful father and how his death had devasted the couple's children. I had also anticipated that Darla would be dressed more conservatively than when I had met her or in the many photos I had seen of her. She had adopted the soccer mom next door look in slacks, a blouse, and flats.

After Darla Esposito was sworn in as a witness and had given her name to the jury, Robin Polk started asking about Henry Esposito.

Darla told the jury they had been married fifteen years and then asked Darla to tell the jury about her family.

She looked over at the jury as I was sure Polk had coached her to do.

When asked, Darla told the jury they had two children. Henry Jr., who was fourteen years old, and Andrea, who was twelve.

I knew what was coming next and, as I expected, Polk had Darla tell the jury that Esposito was a loving father, who spent quality time with their children.

Darla pulled a tissue from her hand. I thought that had been rehearsed as well. Over the next five minutes Darla told the jury that Esposito coached their son's soccer team and bought their daughter a horse, took her to lessons each week and horse shows on weekends. Darla told the jury that their daughter had become a champion equestrian.

Knowing none of the jurors could afford a horse, I wasn't sure whether Polk was making points.

After spending that time to persuade the jury that Henry Esposito had been a great father and made a difference in the life of their children, Polk moved on to asking questions about Hope.

"Did there come a time in your marriage when a problem arose?" Polk asked.

Darla turned and looked at Hope. "Yes, two years ago I discovered that the defendant had seduced my husband."

Hope bowed her head. I could have objected, but the jury had already heard the s word and I thought I might be able to use Darla's accusation to my advantage.

Polk asked Darla how she learned that Hope had seduced Esposito.

Darla said she became suspicious when Henry became less available to coach their son's soccer team and go with their daughter to horse shows. She also claimed he had grown distant in their relationship. When Darla asked him what the problem was, he told her he was working more than before.

Darla's eyes turned red, and she started sniffing and wiping her nose. If this was a planned act, I thought she was doing a good job and I could tell she was an empathetic witness. She went on and told the jury that one night she picked up her husband's phone and found photos of Hope naked. She had sent text messages with photos.

I looked over at the jurors, who looked to be paying close attention to Darla's testimony.

When she confronted Esposito, she testified that he claimed the girl in the photos would not leave him alone.

"What happened after that?" Polk asked.

Darla told the jury she discovered that Henry had an apartment, and the defendant was not the only woman he was seeing at the apartment. At that point, she went to her lawyer, and she filed for divorce. "The defendant and other women had destroyed what had been our happy marriage."

"Did your ex-husband attempt to rewrite his will?"

I quickly stood and objected to the question, but Judge Foster overruled my objection.

"Yes, I found a handwritten document that he wrote as his revised will," Darla answered.

"Did anything in your husband's will surprise you?"

"Yes, in the handwritten will, he attempted to leave five hundred thousand dollars to the defendant. I immediately contacted my lawyer to contest the gift to one of the two women who had killed him. I was told the will wasn't valid since he had not signed it."

I rose and objected. As expected, Judge Foster sustained the objection, but the point had been made to the jury.

"I have no further questions your Honor."

Darla had served the purpose for which Polk had called her. She had told the jury that Henry Esposito had been a wonderful husband and father until Hope Riley seduced him. My job was to show the jury through Darla that her ex-husband was a child predator and a creep.

I turned and looked at Judge Foster, not sure if she planned to take a break. She said, "Ms. Sanchez you can cross-examine."

I started by asking Darla about her career because I wanted the jury to know she was successful in her own right. *Dallas-Fort Worth Magazine* had put her on the cover and called her a self-help guru. Polk stood and objected, claiming Darla's career was irrelevant.

Judge Foster looked down at me. Then she said she would allow the question.

Darla confirmed she had been on the cover of the magazine, and I brought out a copy of the magazine and she testified that she didn't remember the exact title. But she did remember that her photograph had been on the cover of the magazine."

"And you gave up your successful career to raise your children, didn't you?"

Polk stood again and objected. This time Judge Foster allowed Darla to answer the question but directed me to move on.

"Yes," Darla answered. I wanted to devote my time to my children and helping less fortunate children in our community."

"You testified that your husband attempted to rewrite his will but failed to sign it. Isn't it true that you were aware he attempted to rewrite his will before his death?"

Darla wet her lips and then answered. "Yes, Henry told me he had rewritten his will."

"Isn't it true, Mrs. Esposito, that in his rewritten will, Henry left none of his estate to you?"

Darla smirked and I hoped the jury was seeing her facial expressions while answering these questions.

"Yes, that is true, but he left almost his entire estate in a trust for our children."

"In your husband's will that you probated, he left his entire estate to you, isn't that true?"

"Yes," Darla answered and then strangely glanced at her watch as if she had an important meeting scheduled.

I decided to move on. I approached the lectern and put a photograph on the screen for the witness and jury to see.

"Mrs. Esposito, do you recognize the girl in the photograph."

"I am not sure."

I looked over at the jury. They recognized that Hope was the girl in the photo. Darla Esposito knew it also. Hope looked like the innocent fifteen-year-old girl she had been before Henry Esposito changed her appearance.

"Mrs. Esposito, take one more look at the photograph. Can you tell me who the girl is?"

Darla must have sensed she was losing points with the jury. She replied, "It looks like the defendant when she was a younger girl."

"Mrs. Esposito, did you know this photograph was taken of Hope during the talent show your ex-husband judged?"

From Darla's look I thought that tidbit may have taken her by surprise, and when I looked over at the jurors, many of their faces showed their surprise.

"Mrs. Esposito, you say the girl in this photograph seduced your forty-five-year-old ex-husband?"

"Yes."

"Isn't it true that your ex-husband had a thing for younger women and girls?"

"I wouldn't say that."

"You were one of the younger women he went after, isn't that true?"

"I was younger yes."

"Hope wasn't the only teenage girl your ex-husband had sex with, was she?"

"I don't know."

She knew and I wasn't going to let her get away with that answer.

I spent the next ten minutes getting Darla to admit her husband found girls holding guns to be erotic. As expected, she admitted he had taken numerous photos and videos of her in sexy clothes and naked holding guns. The jury seemed quite interested in Esposito's fetish.

At one point Polk objected, but since Esposito had been shot on the same day he had the girls pose with guns, Judge Foster let me continue the questioning.

"Did you become aware that the police were investigating your ex-husband for having sex with teenage girls?"

"Yes, he told me the police were investigating him."

"He also told you that a teenage girl's mother had called the police, isn't that true?"

"Yes."

Her answer showed she knew Hope wasn't the only girl her husband was abusing. I thought about pressing the point and decided against it, thinking that Darla might respond that she assumed it was Hope's mother who had notified the police."

"You testified that your ex-husband left five hundred thousand dollars in a handwritten will to Hope Riley."

"Yes."

"You thought that gave Hope the motive to kill your ex-husband, right?"

"Yes."

"When you divorced, you demanded that your ex-husband buy an insurance policy with you as the beneficiary, isn't that true?"

"Yes."

"And what was the amount of the proceeds from the insurance policy?"

"Five million dollars."

As if she anticipated where I was going with this line of questioning, Darla Esposito quickly added, "But, I wasn't there when your client murdered my ex-husband."

"Did you ever speak with Hope Riley or her friend Amber Davis?"

"Yes, when I found out what was going on I met both of them and told them both to leave my husband alone."

"That was before you started divorce proceedings against your husband?"

"Yes."

"What did the teenage girls say?" I asked.

"I don't recall."

"Did they say they would stop seeing your husband?"

"No."

"Before or after you spoke to the two girls, did you tell your husband to stop having sex with teenage girls?"

"Many times."

"What did he say?"

Darla was silent for a moment, then I saw her eyes tear up. I thought immediately that she was faking it for the jury.

"Each time, he promised he would stop having sex with other women," she gasped while taking a tissue to wipe her face.

"Did he ever stop?"

"Sadly, he didn't. I guess the women were too tempting for him."

"You mean teenage girls in high school?"

"No, he was obsessed with sex. The age didn't matter."

"Was it after you learned the police were investigating your husband that you demanded he buy a five-million-dollar life insurance policy?"

"I don't recall which happened first. It was in our divorce settlement."

I had read the divorce settlement. I picked it up and turned to the page addressing life insurance and read it to Darla Esposito.

"The father shall maintain life insurance, a death benefit equal to, or exceeding, $5,000,000, naming the mother as sole beneficiary for as long as the father has a child support obligation."

"You were the sole beneficiary of the life insurance policy, true?"

"Yes."

"But your ex-husband could cancel the policy when your children were grown, isn't that true?"

"Yes, that is what the agreement says."

"Mrs. Esposito, if you really believe that Hope seduced your ex-husband, don't you also believe it was his responsibility as the forty-five-year-old adult to say no to her?"

Darla Esposito's eyes slowly closed and reopened. I thought she might cry for the jury again. "Yes, Henry should have said no right from the start."

When I sat down, Judge Foster announced a break for lunch.

CHAPTER 40

Gabriela

After lunch, Judge Foster spoke from the bench and asked the bailiff to bring the jury back in. I stood with my see-through shield on as the jury came back in the courtroom and took their seats, still spread out from one another.

"Ms. Polk, you may call your next witness."

"The State calls Vera Anderson."

I had seen on the witness list that Vera Anderson was the dispatcher who had taken Emma Riley's call. I didn't understand why Robin Polk thought it was necessary to have the dispatcher testify. I thought she might introduce the audio recording that had been made of the call. When Vera Anderson testified about the call without introducing the recording, I objected. Robin Polk said she wasn't sure what had happened to the recording. To my surprise Judge Polk overruled my objection.

I knew what Emma had told me and I planned to use it in my cross-examination.

I started by asking how many years Vera Anderson had worked as a dispatcher for the Dallas police.

"I've been a dispatcher for five years."

"And isn't it true that all calls to Dallas police dispatchers are recorded? And Emma Riley's call was recorded, isn't that true?"

"Yes."

"Isn't it true that Emma Riley told you her daughter had called her and said that her friend Amber had accidently shot Henry Esposito?"

"I don't remember her exact words."

I turned to Judge Foster. "Your Honor, we need the actual recording, not what this witness conveniently doesn't remember."

"I agree," Judge Foster replied. "Ms. Polk, I want you to produce the actual recording of the Mrs. Riley's conversation with the dispatcher."

"Your Honor, may we adjourn to your chambers?" Polk asked.

I was curious why Polk wanted to speak in private. It didn't take long to find out.

"Your Honor, I am not certain we have the recording of the call."

"How can that be?" I asked, thinking this was an example of Robin Polk's misconduct.

"Your Honor, we have only recently discovered that in April, investigative data was deleted, including data on the investigation of this case. This investigation data loss has not yet been made public."

"Your Honor, how could a police department as professional as the Dallas Police Department lose evidence that was logged onto a server?"

"That's a good question," Judge Foster said.

"Your Honor, it happened. We don't know how it happened," Polk responded.

"May I assume you have lost all the videos and photographs Henry Esposito took of young girls, including Hope and Amber?" I asked.

Robin Polk threw open her arms with palms up and said, "Yes, I am afraid Esposito's photos and videos are gone also."

I stood, my voice rising with every word, I said. "Your Honor, this is too incredible to be believed. Robin Polk has a reputation for prosecutorial misconduct, but this tops anything I have ever heard."

Judge Foster stared at me. "Ms. Sanchez, you will not accuse the assistant district attorney of prosecutorial misconduct. But Ms. Polk, I am at a loss to understand what has happened."

"We are trying to figure that out ourselves, Your Honor. We think it happened when an IT employee was supposed to move data from online storage to the city's physical drive. It doesn't matter at this point; the evidence is gone and I've been told the chances of it being recovered are nil."

I stood again. "Your Honor, I move to dismiss the charges against Hope Riley. This is a travesty that makes defending her impossible."

Just last week I had seen an article in the Dallas newspaper. The headline was: "Dallas DA Says Loss of Investigation Data May Impact Criminal Trials." I didn't think anything of the article until it turned out that Hope Riley's investigative file had been lost. I had read that the deleted files included audio, video, images, and other evidence.

Would Robin Polk delete investigation data that was helpful to my client? I didn't trust her.

When we returned to the courtroom, I started to ask Vera Anderson why she could not produce the recording of her conversation with Emma Riley. Polk objected, and Judge Foster sustained the objection. I shook my head and sat down and slumped in my chair.

After a break, Robin Polk called officer Randall Grayson to testify.

A handsome, well-built police sergeant walked by me and stood before the clerk. After Grayson was sworn in and seated, Robin Polk started her direct examination.

Polk started by having Sergeant Grayson tell the jury about his employment with the Dallas Police Department and his experience. Then she had him tell the jury about his degree in criminal justice from the University of North Texas and his experience investigating murder cases.

After a few more minutes, Polk finally turned to the case. Officer Grayson testified that he had been asked to investigate Henry Esposito's shooting in November 2019.

"Please tell the jury how you became involved?" Polk asked.

"Certainly," Grayson responded. "May I refer to my notes?"

Polk turned to see if I objected. I had seen the notes and I knew I had no legitimate objection to Grayson referring to them.

"When did you first become involved in the Esposito shooting investigation?"

"It was the evening of November sixteenth, twenty-nineteen. A dispatcher notified me that a lady named Emma Riley was on the telephone and had reported that her daughter Hope had called from a car and that Amber Davis and she had accidently shot Henry Esposito and that they had taken his car and were driving to Miami."

"What did you do?" Polk asked.

"I asked Ms. Riley where her daughter was now, and she told me she had called from somewhere in Louisiana."

"Did Ms. Riley provide you with any additional details?"

"Only that the two girls had taken Henry Esposito's car and that she had told her daughter to come home and report to the police what had happened. After we hung up, I called Mrs. Esposito, who advised me that her husband had been living in an upscale apartment in uptown Dallas. I called emergency services and told them to meet us at the apartment and took a crime team to the apartment."

Officer Grayson described arriving at Esposito's apartment, where he met the Dallas Fire Rescue team that had been dispatched to the apartment. They went into the apartment together and a member of the rescue team advised him that Henry Esposito was dead.

Over the next few minutes, Polk guided the policeman through what he and his team had found. When Grayson described the scene, Polk introduced a gruesome photo of Esposito lying face down with blood all over him and his bed. I objected, but Judge Foster allowed the photo to be shown to the jury and admitted into evidence.

Grayson continued his testimony, telling the jury he had found Esposito's empty wallet with no cash or credit cards and noted that his BMW was missing. After Polk spent more time having Grayson describe the scene, she asked what happened after that.

Grayson testified that he received a call from the Baton Rouge police department, who said they were holding the girls and had done a video interview. "They told us both girls had confessed to killing Henry Esposito."

Polk asked permission to play Hope's video confession to the jury. Over the next few minutes, jurors watched as Hope told the Baton Rouge police officer that she and Amber had shot Henry Esposito. First, she said they had shot him in self-defense. When the police officer reminded her that Esposito was on his stomach, Hope changed her story and said they had accidently shot him. I could tell the video had seriously hurt our defense even though, despite coaxing from the police officer, at no time in the video did Hope say they had shot him and intended to kill him.

After playing the video, Polk told Judge Foster she had no further questions.

Judge Foster looked over at me. "You may cross-examine Ms. Sanchez."

Police officers are notoriously antagonistic toward defendants, but during his direct examination, Grayson had not exaggerated or bent the facts to hurt Hope. So I hoped he had stronger negative feelings about Henry Esposito than he did about Hope. With that in mind, I thought he would be less likely to do battle with me. I wanted to deal with the so-called confession right away.

"Officer Grayson, what Ms. Polk claims was Hope's confession wasn't really a confession, was it?"

He thought for a moment and then answered: "Ms. Sanchez, I would say what she told the officer speaks for itself. You don't need to put a label on it."

That answer didn't help us.

"If it speaks for itself officer, wouldn't you say that Hope was just making up stories until she satisfied the Baton Rouge police officer?"

"It is true she told more than one version of events."

"And in the video, she stopped when she had satisfied him, right?"

"Yes."

That was better.

Hope had told me the detective had interrogated her for more than two hours before he turned on the video camera, so I asked: "Do you know how many hours before what the jury saw on video, he had been interrogating her or what he told her during that time?"

"No."

"In your years of experience, isn't it true you have found that at some point in an interrogation, the accused simply tells the officer what he wants to hear?"

"That happens, but not very often."

I had learned that Grayson was the lead investigating Henry Esposito, so I started asking about that investigation. "Officer Grayson, were you investigating Henry Esposito for trafficking and exploiting teenage girls?"

Polk stood quickly and objected.

"On what grounds, Ms. Polk," Judge Foster asked.

"It is beyond the scope of his direct examination. If Ms. Sanchez wants to ask that question, she can call officer Grayson as a witness."

Judge Foster frowned and invited us to come to her bench.

She spoke softly, not wanting the jury to hear her. "Ms. Polk, we have a serious backlog of trials, meaning we have no time to waste," she said while leaning down toward Polk. "Do you want me to waste the court's time and officer Grayson's time by making Ms. Sanchez call him during the defense case?"

Polk knew when to keep her mouth shut. But given her strides back to her counsel table, I could tell she was not happy.

"Yes," Grayson answered. "We had started an investigation of Henry Esposito."

"What prompted the investigation?"

Grayson looked at Polk before answering. I assumed he expected her to object to the question. When she didn't, he answered.

"A mother called and later brought her teenage daughter to meet with us. The mother claimed the fourteen-year-old daughter had been having sex with a wealthy man at his Dallas apartment. She also told us her daughter knew of other girls who the wealthy man molested. The mother showed us a necklace she said the wealthy man had given her daughter."

I knew that because of the girl's age, Grayson would not refer to her by name.

"How did you figure out the wealthy man was Henry Esposito?"

Grayson looked over at the jury. Several jurors stared at him while listening. I looked at Judge Foster. She was leaning in and listening intently and looking at me and then at Grayson. Perhaps the judge shared Grayson's contempt for Henry Esposito. I hoped the jurors felt the same.

"The girl gave us the address of the apartment and the apartment number, and we determined it was Henry Esposito's apartment."

"Did you believe the young girl?"

"Yes, she was credible, and she had obviously been inside Henry's Esposito's apartment. She was able to describe each room, including the furniture. She also described for us a scar Esposito had on his stomach, meaning she had seen him with without a shirt."

"What else did you learn from the girl and her mother?"

"We asked her to give us the names of other teenage girls so we could confirm her story."

"Did the young girl give you other names?"

"Yes, and the defendant was one of the girls she named. When we spoke to the defendant, she denied any involvement with Mr. Esposito other than he had judged her high school talent show."

"What happened after that?"

"By the time we interviewed each of the other girls, each denied that Esposito had sex with them or had given them money or expensive gifts, and the mother who brought to our attention that Esposito had molested her called and told us her daughter said she had made up the story. We didn't believe her. We thought Esposito or one of his friends had paid the mother so her daughter would change her story. We also thought Esposito, or his friends, had either paid or threatened other teenagers to not accuse him. It brought our investigation to a halt."

"Did you try to get a search warrant for Esposito's apartment?"

"No."

"After Mr. Esposito died, did you and other Dallas police officers go through what was on his computer?"

"Yes. He had attempted to delete the photographs and videos, but our forensic computer experts were able to retrieve hundreds of videos and photographs he had deleted."

"With regard to the teenage girls, what did you find?"

Grayson once again turned and looked at the jurors. "We found hundreds of photos and videos of young girls having sex with Esposito, having sex with each other, or just stimulating themselves on the camera for him."

"Was Hope Riley in any of the videos or photographs?" I asked.

Grayson cleared his throat before answering. "Yes, she was in many of Esposito's photos and videos."

"Was Amber Davis in any of the videos and photographs?"

"Yes, like the defendant, she appears in many of the photographs and videos."

"And were Amber and Hope in any photographs and videos together?"

"Yes, they are together in several photos and videos."

"Are those photographs and video available now?" I knew the answer, but I wanted to make sure the jury heard it.

Grayson shifted in his seat. "No, they were apparently deleted in the data loss." He shook his head in disgust. "I've been told the photos and videos were all lost while an employee was transferring files to a new network."

"How did that happen?"

"I have no idea. I know the loss of terabytes of data is being investigated."

"Was the employee who lost the data charged with a crime or at least fired?"

Grayson shook his head again.

"I believe at least one employee was fired. The loss of data has been in the news and affected the evidence we have for trials including videos and photos."

"And your forensic computer experts are not able to retrieve the photos and videos?"

"I was told they are permanently lost."

I decided to wrap up my cross-examination with a few more questions.

"Officer Grayson, isn't it true Hope Riley did not shoot the gun that killed Henry Esposito?"

"That is true. Her friend shot the gun."

"You have no evidence that Hope Riley gave Amber Davis the gun, isn't that true?"

Grayson squirmed in his seat.

"Ms. Davis told us Hope Riley gave her the gun and nodded for her to fire it."

I was not aware that Amber Davis had changed her story once again. My next question was anticipating an instruction I expected Judge Foster to give the jury.

"Officer Grayson, the only evidence you have suggesting that Hope Riley had anything to do with her friend shooting Henry Esposito is Amber Davis's statement that Hope nodded after she pulled the trigger and there was no bullet in the chamber, and then she pulled the trigger again."

"Well, the defendant was there at the time. The defendant tried to get away in Mr. Esposito's car."

I interrupted. "But other than being there, the only evidence you have that Hope Riley had anything to do with the shooting is Amber Davis saying Hope nodded, isn't that true?"

In a notable monotone voice, Grayson answered, "Yes."

"Officer Grayson, when Amber Davis pulled the trigger the first time and there was no bullet in the chamber, she would have heard a click, right?"

"The sound from the nine-millimeter would have been a click. I can't tell you whether she heard it."

"And isn't it true that the semi-automatic gun will not load a round automatically after the click?"

"Yes."

"That means Amber would have had to have pulled the slide back with her hand and let it go forward before firing the gun with a bullet loaded."

Having never shot a semi-automatic pistol, I wasn't sure I was using the right terminology and I wasn't sure the jury understood that Amber needed to pull the slide with a loaded clip to chamber the first bullet. I decided to put a photo on the screen for the jury to see what I was asking. Polk objected as I expected she would, and Judge Foster overruled her objection.

"Officer Grayson, describe for the jury what you see in this photo."

"A person is pulling the slide back to its rearmost position, which will chamber a round the person can then shoot."

"And isn't true that after Amber fired the first shot, she would have had to pull the trigger to fire a second shot and pull the trigger again to fire a third shot?"

"Yes, she had to manually pull the trigger for the gun to fire."

"Is there any way she could have pulled the trigger a second and a third time without realizing what she was doing?"

Polk objected and Judge Foster sustained the objection. But I had gotten my point across to the jury.

I didn't want to aggravate Grayson, but I felt compelled to ask him a tough question. "If you had obtained a search warrant, you would have the evidence you just described you found after his death."

"Only if Mr. Esposito had not destroyed the evidence first. He knew we were investigating him."

"And you've testified that you were investigating Mr. Esposito for trafficking young teenage girls, isn't that true?"

I anticipated an objection from Robin Polk, but she stayed in her seat.

Grayson seemed anxious to answer the question, so before Polk could object, he answered, "Yes, as I said earlier, we were investigating Henry Esposito for trafficking young teenage girls."

"And even though Hope had denied it, you were investigating his trafficking Hope Riley. Isn't that true?"

"Yes, when I interviewed her, I didn't believe what she told me. I believed she was a potential victim."

Before this case, I knew nothing about guns. I had never shot a gun. But when I learned that the pistol Amber had shot three times was a Smith and Wesson M&P Shield EZ Pistol, I did a Google search and found something I thought might explain why Amber fired the pistol three times in rapid succession.

"Officer Grayson, did you discover what kind of gun Amber Davis shot three times?"

"Yes."

"It was a pistol, not a revolver, right?" I asked.

"That is correct."

"And isn't it true that a pistol is easier to shoot than a revolver?"

Grayson shook his head. "Yes, a pistol is easier to shoot."

"And the make of the pistol Amber Davis shot was a Smith and Wesson EZ Pistol, isn't that true?"

"Yes, that was the pistol."

"And EZ stands for easy meaning easy to shoot, isn't that true?"

"Yes, that is true."

I showed Grayson a photo of the Smith and Wesson M&P EZ Pistol and had him tell the jury that it was the same make and model of the gun with which Amber Davis had shot and killed Henry Esposito. Then I put the photo on the screen so the jury could see the pistol.

"Are you aware Smith and Wesson issued a safety recall on the M&P Shield EZ Pistol?"

Grayson looked confused.

"No, I am not aware."

I showed him a Smith and Wesson recall notice, which was issued because of a crack in the hammer of two pistols, which caused the pistol to potentially have multiple discharges without depressing the trigger. He turned his head to the side, which I interpreted to mean that the recall had taken him by surprise. When I asked him about the recall, Grayson pointed out the one weakness in my argument.

"Ms. Sanchez, this recall notice is aimed at pistols that were manufactured between March first and October thirty-first of twenty-twenty. Amber Davis shot Henry Esposito in twenty-nineteen."

"But do you acknowledge that it is possible that the EZ pistol had multiple discharges without Amber Davis pulling the trigger?"

Grayson sighed. "I seriously doubt that happened. Even in the recall notice you sent me, Smith and Wesson had only identified two instances where that happened."

"Isn't it also possible that because the pistol is easy to shoot, Amber Davis could have panicked and pulled the trigger three times?"

"That is possible."

I wanted to get Grayson to agree to one more point.

"Officer Grayson, isn't it possible that Henry Esposito loaded the pistol before Hope and Amber arrived and wanted to be shot before he was arrested?"

Robin Polk was up in a flash. I had anticipated her objection. When it was my turn, I pointed out that Darla Esposito had testified that her ex-husband had never used a loaded gun when he had her pose for videos and photos. Someone put bullets in the gun. If it was Henry Esposito, then he wanted the girls to shoot him. As we went back and forth, I also made the point that if Henry Esposito committed suicide, the insurance company would not pay out on his five-million-dollar policy.

Judge Foster ruled that it called for speculation, but I had planted a seed for the jury to consider.

"Officer Grayson," I continued. "You don't know who put the bullets into the pistol, do you?"

"That is correct. But I know who shot the pistol, and I know who confessed to being by her side." I tried to interrupt him, but he continued. "And I know who took his money and his car and left Henry Esposito in a pool of blood."

I had just asked one question too many and had given Grayson a chance to bury my client. I saw no way to make things better for us, so I sat down. Robin Polk smiled and raised her thumb to Grayson. That was all I needed to see.

As expected, Judge Foster adjourned for the day. I expected in the morning Robin Polk would call the medical examiner and then most likely call her star witness, Amber Davis. I had lots of work to do anticipating Amber Davis would lie on the stand. I thought I was ready, but I wasn't sure how Davis would place the blame on Hope.

Chapter 41

Gabriela

Contrary to what I had planned, when I got home, before eating, I made a lemon drop martini and drank it. I liked how it tasted. Then I made another and drank it. I justified drinking because it relaxed me and made it easier to go to sleep and stay asleep until morning.

Each day thereafter I came home and told myself I did not need to drink to relieve the tension I felt. But that did not stop me. I made and drank two lemon drop martinis. I continued to justify my drinking by saying the martinis tasted good and drinking them helped me recover from the stress of the trial that day. Drinking helped me sleep and I needed the sleep each night to be ready for trial the next day. Thankfully my father never asked if I was drinking and I never had to tell him.

As expected, at ten o'clock sharp, Dr. Richard Ortega walked to the plexiglass-protected witness stand and was administered the oath. After saying, "I do," Dr. Ortega sat behind the glass, put on his glasses, and started looking at papers in front of him. I was surprised by his attire. He wore a dark blue shirt with a blue striped tie that probably had gone out of style years before. He wore dark horn-rimmed glasses that did little to enhance his image.

Polk asked him to state his name and then asked how he was employed. He took off his glasses and told the jury he had been the chief medical examiner for Dallas County since 2001. For the next fifteen minutes, Polk asked Ortega about his education and his experience. She then had Ortega explain that his office conducts inquests to determine manner and cause of death and that one of the main tools his office uses is an autopsy. He said he had testified numerous times in the courtroom.

Polk then asked how his office got involved in making autopsies and how the office generated an autopsy report.

Next, Polk asked Ortega if he took photographs and made drawings of the body, called a body diagram, to better explain the autopsy. She started putting the photographs, drawings, and the autopsy report on the screen.

Ortega advised the jury that Henry Esposito was six feet two inches and weighed 178 pounds. He was a White male.

I was bored with the level of detail. I felt sure the jury just wanted Ortega to say that Esposito had been shot three times at close range in the chest and abdomen and that the manner of death was homicide. Finally, Ortega got to that testimony and Polk advised everyone she had no more questions.

I knew that in most cases, cross-examination of a pathologist is useless and having watched YouTube videos of other defense lawyers cross-examining Dr. Ortega, I learned that was certainly true. I planned to ask only a very few questions.

In his direct examination, Ortega had never testified where the three bullets had entered Esposito's body. I got him to admit that Esposito was lying on his back, not his stomach, as he was shot.

"Did you study the trajectory of the bullets entering Mr. Esposito's body?"

"Yes."

"Was the person who shot Mr. Esposito, standing, sitting, or lying down next to him?"

"Standing."

"Did you estimate the height of the person who shot Mr. Esposito?"

"We did. We believe the shooter was standing and he or she was somewhere between five feet four inches and five feet six inches."

I looked back at Hope. She was taller than me and at least five feet ten inches.

Then I asked, "Dr. Ortega, isn't it true that when you conclude that the manner of death was homicide, that term does not imply criminal intent?"

"Yes, that is true," Ortega answered.

"It is possible that the person who shot Mr. Esposito did not know the gun she shot was loaded, isn't that true?"

I expected Polk to object, but she remained seated.

"That is possible," Ortega replied.

I wanted to get one more important detail from him.

"Did you determine a time of death?" I asked.

He looked down at his notes.

"It was approximately four-thirty p.m."

"Did Mr. Esposito die immediately from a gunshot wound?"

"Yes."

It was time to quit while I was ahead.

After a break, Robin Polk announced her next witness. "The state calls Amber Davis."

I had anticipated Polk would have made sure Davis looked like the picture of innocence, but as she walked to the witness stand, I thought I was seeing an audition for Dorothy in a remake of the Wizard of Oz. The only things missing were the pigtails and Toto.

Davis's hair was in a ponytail. She wore a white blouse with a black tie around the collar, a green cardigan sweater, and a blue plaid skirt. It almost looked like a school uniform. The only thing missing were the knee-high socks.

I looked over at Hope, whose mouth was wide open. I expected she would be even more surprised by her friend's testimony.

After taking the oath and stating her name, she looked at Robin Polk, who began her questioning.

Polk started by asking Amber to tell the jury about her home life. I objected on the grounds that it was irrelevant, but Judge Foster let her answer.

Amber told the jury her father had abandoned her family when she was a little girl, leaving her mother with no money and no job to care for the children. Amber described how her mother had tried hard, but she couldn't hold a job and she had become addicted to drugs.

I could tell she was making points with the jury, which was what Polk hoped to accomplish.

Amber described taking care of her little brother and having no money for food or anything. After her mother was arrested, she and her brother had been placed into a group home in Dallas. It was so overcrowded that neither of them had beds. She told the jury she frequently slept in a chair in the office and her brother slept on the floor or on a cot. While they were at the group home, a mentor heard her sing. She believed in Amber and recommended that she go to school for the performing and visual arts. She also found a foster home for Amber and her brother.

After fifteen minutes of making Amber appear to be the poor, saintly girl that her outfit displayed, Polk finally moved to questions about how Amber met Henry Esposito.

"How did you meet the defendant?"

"During my first week at high school I met Hope. She was kind of a tomboy, so she stood out from the other girls. We became friends and in a couple of weeks we became lovers."

I had thought Hope and Amber were more than just friends, but Hope had denied it.

How did you meet Henry Esposito?" Polk asked.

"My friend, Hope, asked me if I wanted to earn some money. I asked what she had in mind."

"What did she tell you?"

"She said that the man who had judged our talent show was looking for girls our age who wanted to earn some money," Amber responded. "My mother was in jail, and I had no money, so I told her I was interested."

Hope wrote a note: "BS, she's lying."

I wanted to reply that it was just the first of many lies to come, but I wanted to pay attention to the questioning.

"What happened next?" Polk asked.

"Hope took me to Mr. Esposito's apartment. Mr. Esposito said he remembered me from the talent show and that he had friends in the recording business who would like to meet me and that they would pay me to perform for them."

"What did you say."

"I was excited about the opportunity. I knew that Mr. Esposito had introduced Hope to people in the movie industry. I told Mr. Esposito I would gladly sing at any events and prove I could become a recording star."

"What happened next?"

"When we were alone, Hope told me that Mr. Esposito's friends would pay me at least two hundred dollars for companionship and they would also give me opportunities to meet people in the music business."

"So, you understood the defendant had recruited you to have sex with—"

Before Polk could finish, I rose to my feet and objected.

"Your Honor, she's leading the witness." I wanted to add there was no evidence that Hope had recruited Amber, but I knew that objection would just highlight the word for the jury. The more Amber testified, the more I sensed that Hope would have to testify.

Judge Foster replied through her plexiglass shield. "Ms. Polk, please revise your question so it is not leading the witness."

Polk smiled. She had said enough to coach her witness.

"So, Ms. Davis, what did you understand after you had met with Mr. Esposito and talked about it with the defendant."

"I understood that Hope had recruited me on behalf of Mr. Esposito to have sex with him and his friends and in return they would pay me, and they would help me become a recording artist."

That must have been an answer Polk had rehearsed with Amber. She wanted to make sure Amber said Hope had recruited her.

"When did you first have sex with one of Mr. Esposito's friends?"

"I can't tell you the exact date, but I believe it was in November or December of twenty-eighteen. I remember it was cold the first time I went to Mr. Esposito's apartment and met one of his friends."

"What did the defendant tell you to expect about that first night?"

"Hope said it was a party." Amber paused again as if looking for some coaching. She finally continued. "Hope said I would be paid five hundred dollars to mingle with Mr. Esposito's friends."

"What happened?"

Amber took several breaths while her hands were trembling. She looked down at her hands and placed them on her lap. I thought it seemed too rehearsed to be real.

"A man I didn't know escorted me into one of Mr. Esposito's bedrooms and started unbuttoning his shirt. When I asked what he was doing, he told me to strip, and he put five one-hundred-dollar bills on the table by the bed."

"What did you do?"

Amber swallowed a couple of times and her chin dropped. In a weak voice she finally responded, "My brother and I needed the money. We were living in a foster home and never had any money of our own. I had never seen five one-hundred-dollar bills. I was willing to take the money because we needed it for survival. I let the man have sex with me."

"Amber," Polk responded. "Please repeat your answer. This time more loudly so the jurors can hear you."

I had heard every word of the answer, and I was sure the jury had also heard it. Polk wanted the answer to be branded in the jury's mind. I listened as she repeated what she had said, this time more loudly as she wiped her eye.

"What did you do after that first night?"

"I used the money to purchase school supplies for me and my brother and to purchase some clothes for each of us."

"What happened after that first incident?" Polk asked.

"Hope pressured me to go back to another Esposito party."

"What happened at the party?

"Another man I didn't know started talking to me. He told me he was a music producer and that Esposito had given him a recording I had made. I was excited because I knew that any singer needed a music producer to help with the production process."

"What happened?" Polk asked.

"We talked for about thirty minutes. I was drinking wine at the time. He finally invited me to the same bedroom I had been in before. There was another girl already in the room. I didn't know her. The music producer put five one-hundred-dollar bills in an envelope and handed it to me. He told me he liked threesomes."

"Did you engage in the threesome?"

Amber straightened her back and shifted in her seat.

"I needed the money for my brother."

Amber failed to mention that she preferred having sex with girls and women. I looked over at the jury and, as I expected, Amber was scoring major points with them.

"Did Henry Esposito ever pay you to have sex with him?"

"Yes, many times."

"Did the defendant know Esposito was paying you to have sex with him?"

"Yes, I showed her the money."

"What did she say."

"Hope didn't say anything, but I could tell she was upset that Mr. Esposito had sex with me without including her. She wanted me all to herself."

I wanted to call bullshit. If Hope wanted Amber all to herself, why would she recruit Amber to have sex with Esposito and his friends for money?

Polk finally got to the day of the shooting.

"Please tell the jury how you ended up at Henry Esposito's apartment the day he was shot."

"It was Hope's seventeenth birthday. A week before, she told me that Henry Esposito had invited her to his apartment, and he asked if she would bring me with her."

"Please continue," Polk said.

"We took Uber from Hope's apartment to Mr. Esposito's apartment. He gave us alcoholic drinks and he had several presents he gave Hope. After about an hour of talking and watching television, he escorted us into his large bedroom, where he had a video camera set up. He told us to take off our clothes and mentioned that because the police were investigating him, this might be our last time together.

"We did as we were told, and he said he wanted some video and photos of us holding one of his guns and posing for the camera. Hope went to the cabinet. When she returned, she handed a gun to me."

"Let me stop you there," Polk interrupted. "Was this the first time Henry Esposito wanted to shoot video and take photos of you and the defendant holding one of his guns?"

"Oh no. We had done this many times before."

"Did you find it odd and ask what he was doing?"

Amber shuffled in her seat and sat up straight. She looked over at the jury. "The first time he had us pose with one of his guns, I thought it was weird. Afterward, I asked Hope what he was doing, and Hope replied that Esposito was a gun collector and for some reason he liked to create videos and take photos of women and girls holding guns. I still thought it was weird, but I went along with it."

"What happened when you were holding the gun?"

"As we had done before, Hope nodded, and I pulled the trigger. Like before I heard a click. Hope nodded again and I pulled the trigger a second time and this time a bullet discharged. I panicked and heard the gun discharge a second time and a third time. I looked and Mr. Esposito was covered in blood, and I was covered in blood."

I had always wondered why Amber had said she pulled the trigger when Hope nodded. I thought it was to set up the whole shooting as an accident, giving the jury a reason to find Hope not guilty. Polk obviously had seen the potential problem, so Amber's story was about to change.

"Did Hope say why she nodded?" Polk asked.

Amber looked at the jury. "She said she wanted him dead because he was molesting her and so the two of us could be together."

I heard a juror gasp, which was never a good sign.

Hope almost broke her pen forcefully writing "Liar."

In some ways Amber's testimony reminded me of "fake news." Just like someone saying something happened and the media reporting it even if it wasn't true, Amber could create a story of what happened that day.

Amber continued. "We didn't know what to do. Hope wanted to take Mr. Esposito's car and leave as soon as I could wash up and change clothes. She said that way we could always be together."

Polk nodded. "Was that the reason you left the scene?"

"Yes, I was in a panic. I had shot Mr. Esposito by accident, but Hope had planned it all along. I was worried no one would believe my story. In a panic I agreed to leave the scene in Mr. Esposito's BMW with Hope."

If Amber Davis was lying, she was doing a great job of it. I knew Hope would have a tough time convincing the jury that her story was true.

"Where were you heading in Mr. Esposito's car?"

"Hope suggested we drive to Miami. I went along because I wanted to be with her."

"What was in Miami?"

"I don't know. She said she heard it was a cool place to live and become a fashion model."

"What did you discuss while you were driving?" Polk asked.

"When we were in the car, Hope told me we had to make up a story to use if we got caught," Amber answered. "At first, we talked about that we had found him dead when we arrived. Hope didn't think the police would believe that story based on where he had been shot. We even thought about claiming we had taken the gun from him and shot in self-defense. We decided our better story would be that the gun had gone off by accident."

"Amber, why did you agree to protect the defendant if you got caught?"

Davis flipped her shoulders and then answered. "We were in love. At the time, I wanted to protect her."

She seemed so sincere. It couldn't be real? Or could it? I snuck a peek over at Hope. She was beet red. I had anticipated this kind of testimony from her so-called lover. Hope clearly had not.

"What did you do with the gun?"

"We wiped our prints. Hope put it in Esposito's hand so the police might think he committed suicide."

Polk then had Amber testify about pleading true to a criminally negligent homicide and being sent to a juvenile justice facility. She testified she was working on the Capital and Serious Violent Treatment Program. I objected on grounds that all of her juvenile treatment was irrelevant, but Judge Foster let her continue.

Amber was a good witness who had been coached by Polk on how to persuade the jury. She described the treatment program that had made her realize what she had been doing prior to shooting Henry Esposito was wrong.

Finally, Robin Polk had all that she wanted and told Judge Foster she had no further questions and walked back to the prosecution table.

Judge Foster took a fifteen-minute break, during which I had to decide how to cross-examine the state's star witness. I had been warned that Robin Polk would do anything to win. I had anticipated she would have Amber Davis tell big lies about her friend's involvement in the shooting. Now I had to deal with the lies.

CHAPTER 42

Gabriela

There are two kinds of lying witnesses. The first kind lies because she wants to hurt someone. The second kind lies because she is forced to in order to save herself. Amber was the second kind of liar. To effectively cross-examine Amber, I had to put myself in her shoes and cross-examine her with that in mind.

I started with her background. I wanted to show the jury it was more likely that Amber approached Hope rather than vice versa.

"Ms. Davis, my name is Gabriela Sanchez. I represent Hope Riley and I want to ask you a few questions."

"I know who you are, Ms. Sanchez."

Over the next few minutes, I got Amber to admit that when she had met Hope Riley, she was living in a foster home with her brother and had no money. She said she worried about having money for school supplies.

"Because you needed the money to support you and your brother, you created an online account and became an escort isn't that true?"

She looked over at Robin Polk, apparently expecting Polk to object to the question. When Polk remained silent, Amber answered. "I needed money for my brother and me."

I put up an ad from Backpage. It included a photo of Amber wearing a pair of sky-high silver stilettos. She was only fifteen at the time of the ad and she looked far less innocent than she did now.

"You created this ad, isn't that true?"

She sat up in her chair and paused, as if thinking of some way to deny it was her. Finally, she answered, "Yes."

"And you were able to solicit sex from men for one hundred dollars an hour, isn't that true?"

"Yes."

"You also used your Snapchat account to solicit men for sex, isn't that true?"

"Yes."

I didn't know much about Snapchat, but Hope had told me Amber had set up a Premium Snapchat account to make money. I had searched and found her account before the trial.

"And because you and your brother needed the money, you sold videos and photos of yourself naked on a Premium Snapchat account, and you used Snapcash and Google Wallet to get paid, isn't that true?"

"Yes. As I said before, I needed the money to feed myself and my brother."

I asked to introduce some of Amber's Snapchat Premium photos into evidence and, as expected, Robin Polk objected. Judge Foster sustained the objection, but I was convinced the jury had understood my point.

I moved on.

"You and Hope were very close friends at school, right?"

"We were best friends."

"You did everything together, both at school and away from school, and you wanted Hope to be your girlfriend and lover, isn't that true?"

"Hope was my girlfriend. We loved each other even after she had seduced Henry Esposito."

That was an interesting answer. Amber claimed her lover friend Hope had initiated the relationship with Esposito. She wanted to convey to the jury that Hope wasn't the innocent girl she appeared to be now.

"At the time you were prostituting yourself on social media, you wanted more money and you saw two one-hundred-dollar bills in Hope Riley's purse and asked where she got the money, isn't that true?"

"No, Hope showed me the two one-hundred-dollar bills. She said an older rich guy had given her the money for sex and she could get more whenever she wanted. She asked if I wanted to go to a party and earn two hundred dollars."

"Henry Esposito, and his friends, paid you to have sex with them at least once a week for how many weeks?"

Amber squirmed in her chair. After what seemed like a couple of minutes, she testified that she didn't know how many times Esposito and his friends paid her and then added she also didn't know how many weeks Hope was able to get money from Henry Esposito.

I asked if it was more than ten times, and Amber said it was. I asked if it was over twenty times, and Amber testified that she thought she had had sex with Henry Esposito and his friends about twenty times.

I was able to get Amber to tell the jury that she had been paid over five thousand dollars by Henry Esposito and his friends. Once again, she added on her own that Henry Esposito paid more each visit for Hope.

By that point, it was clear that Robin Polk's strategy was to use Amber to make the jurors neither like nor trust Hope. Sadly, the strategy was working. I believed I had gone as far as reasonable on her sexual activity for money, especially the way she was responding more about Hope than herself.

"Hope and your friends all had smartphones, tablets, and watches, so you took some of the money and bought a new cell phone, tablet, and smart watch, isn't that true?"

"Yes, Hope thought we should both buy cell phones, tablets, and smart watches."

"And you have your smart watch on, is that correct?"

Polk objected, saying it was irrelevant. I responded that it was relevant because on direct examination Amber had testified that she needed the money to take care of herself and her brother. Judge Foster allowed my question.

After the argument, Amber asked me to repeat the question.

"You bought a smart watch with money you were paid to have sex with Mr. Esposito's friends, isn't that true?"

Amber answered while touching the watch on her arm.

"And you bought a smartphone with the money you were paid to have sex with Mr. Esposito's friends, isn't that true?"

Amber squirmed in the witness chair before answering yes.

"You thought it was pretty cool to be photographed with guns, so you posted photos of yourself on social media holding Mr. Esposito's guns, isn't that true?"

Amber's face turned red. I hoped the jury was taking notice she did not feel comfortable answering my questions.

"Yes," she finally answered.

I asked Amber to tell the jury she had made up stories of what happened in the shooting.

"You didn't want to testify against Hope, did you?"

Amber looked over at Hope.

"No, she was my best friend, and we love each other. But she is not Miss Innocent. She took advantage of an older guy and took his money every time she saw him."

"And Ms. Polk told you that you had to testify against her and if you didn't testify, you'd be in a trial just like this one. Isn't that what she told you?"

"Yes."

"You agreed to tell the jury the truth, the whole truth, and nothing but the truth, isn't that true?"

"Yes."

"Your idea of the truth has changed several times, isn't that true?"

I watched as she put her hand on her chin.

"Yes, Hope told me what I should say happened."

I wanted to pursue some of Amber's stories. "You first said you had shot Mr. Esposito three times in self-defense, is that correct?"

"Yes, Hope and I agreed that would be our best story."

"Was that true?"

"No." She looked over at Hope. "We thought the police would not arrest us if I shot in self-defense."

"And another story was you didn't know Esposito's gun was loaded, was that story true?

"Yes."

Amber was either a very accomplished liar or she had been coached very well. I wanted the jury to know that Amber had several stories on what happened. Each story was created for a reason. Her final story was what Robin Polk wanted her to tell the jury. I got her to admit she at first claimed the shooting was self-defense. Next, she claimed she was not aware the gun was loaded. Then, she claimed Hope had nodded, which she had understood to mean she should pull the trigger.

"The prosecutor, Ms. Polk, agreed to treat you as a juvenile, isn't that true?"

"Yes."

Amber was treated as a juvenile when Robin Polk could have tried her as an adult. I had her describe what it had been like to be in juvenile custody. She told the jury she had been able to go to classes until COVID struck. Afterward, she was able to take classes online.

"And, as a juvenile, Ms. Polk has told you that you'll be released from custody and put on parole when you are eighteen years old, isn't that true?"

Amber glanced over at Robin Polk, as if asking how she was supposed to answer the question. Finally, she said, "Ms. Polk told me to cooperate or I would be sent to the adult court system."

"And face going to prison for forty to fifty years, isn't that true?"

"Maybe I was told something like that."

"And by cooperate you had to testify and place the blame for the shooting on Hope. Isn't that true?"

"No. Ms. Polk told me she would treat me as a juvenile if I would tell the truth about the shooting."

I had thought about how I wanted to cross-examine Amber about the shooting. I wanted to slow it down as if in slow motion. I decided to ask her about each time she pulled the trigger.

"According to your story, Hope never told you to pull the trigger, it was just a feeling you had, isn't that what you have said?"

"I said Hope nodded, which I understood meant to pull the trigger."

"And the truth was you pulled the trigger once and you heard a click?"

"Yes."

"You've said that then you pulled the trigger a second time and the gun fired, making a loud noise and a bullet hit Henry Esposito, isn't that true?"

"Yes."

I showed Amber a drawing of the gun and a person firing it. "To fire this weapon, you had to move the safety to the fire position. How did you know you needed to do that to fire the weapon?"

Amber looked confused, like she was trying to remember doing that.

Finally, she answered. "I don't remember."

I showed her another drawing.

"To fire this weapon, you had to use the palm of your hand to pull the slide to its rearmost position and release it to chamber a round. How did you know how to chamber a round?"

Amber shrugged. "I guess I must have seen it in a movie."

"And isn't it also true that you pulled the trigger a third time and the bullet hit Henry Esposito?"

"Yes, but it happened so fast."

"But the gun didn't fire itself. It happened slow enough that you pulled the trigger, isn't that true?"

She gave a sheepish look and finally responded, "Yes."

"And isn't it also true that you pulled the trigger a fourth time and the bullet hit Henry Esposito?"

"Yes, but it happened so fast that I couldn't control what happened."

"Hope never sent you an email or a text message saying she wanted to hurt or kill Henry Esposito, did she?"

Amber's eyes moved up as if she was thinking about whether to lie. She finally answered, "No. But, I knew she wanted us to be together."

I tried to think of other questions to ask. I knew I would not be able to have a Perry Mason moment where Amber admitted Hope wasn't in the room, or if she was had not done anything to cause Amber to fire the weapon and kill Esposito.

"While you were driving to Miami, Hope spoke to her mother, isn't that true?"

Amber shifted again in the witness chair. I hoped the jury noticed.

"Yes, she called her mother."

"And after the call, Hope wanted to return to Dallas and turn herself in to the police, isn't that true?"

"We talked about it and we both decided no one would believe our story."

I wanted to close with a bang and wanted to be able to turn to the jury with a look of disdain I hoped they would feel toward Amber.

"So Miss Davis, I want to summarize what you have told the jury. You have testified that Hope was your best friend and that you loved Hope. Yet, you have alleged in order to receive a better deal from Ms. Polk that your best friend and the girl you loved nodded when you had a gun in your hand and you somehow took the nod to mean you were supposed to pull the trigger of the gun, not once, not twice, and even after a bullet exited and hit Mr. Esposito, not three times, but four times. Did Ms. Polk tell you that if you betrayed your best friend and lover, you could get a better deal?"

Polk was out of her chair objecting in a flash, but I had done the damage I wished to inflict on Amber Davis, and I turned to the jury with the best look of contempt I could muster.

On redirect, Polk focused on getting Amber to put blame on Hope. For at least ten minutes they focused on that. Then, as expected, Polk focused on how the only thing that she had required of Amber was that she tell the truth to the jury. Knowing how many stories Amber had created before the one she told the jury, I didn't think the jury was buying the rehearsed testimony.

With that, the prosecution rested and I was tasked with prepping Hope Davis to deliver a performance I hoped would save her future.

CHAPTER 43

Gabriela

The next morning, after Judge Foster and the jury had been seated, I called Oliva Turner to testify. I saw Robin Polk searching her notes. When she finally looked up, she told the judge Olivia Turner was not on the list of witnesses I had given her. She asked that the jury be excused while we argued whether Olivia Turner would be given permission to testify.

Judge Foster excused the jury and asked us to approach the bench. Before I started forward, I was handed a note: "William Scott says he told Robin Polk you planned to call Olivia Turner as a witness." I made this point to Judge Foster. Polk said she had other objections to the testimony and Judge Foster decided we should examine Olivia Turner without the jury so she could decide whether she should be allowed to testify. Knowing the intense media coverage of the trial, Judge Foster cleared the courtroom and Olivia Turner took her seat in the witness chair.

I hoped she would clear the hurdle and be able to tell the jury what she had told me. During my direct examination, she told Judge Foster exactly what she told me earlier. She testified that Amber had told her in the juvenile detention facility that she had shot and killed a businessman named Henry Esposito and that she never mentioned that Hope was present. I could tell what she said had made an impression on Judge Foster.

When Olivia finished her story. Judge Foster asked if Polk had any questions. Her questions were surprisingly few. All she wanted to know was when Amber had allegedly told her about shooting Henry Esposito. Once she established the approximate date, she sat down. A few minutes later, after Olivia was excused, I found out why.

Polk objected to the testimony on the basis of hearsay and relevancy. I was shocked. How could the testimony not be relevant? She essentially testified that Amber Davis had told her a different story not involving Hope than the one she told the jury. I quickly sorted through the Texas Evidence book on my desk. I found the rule on exceptions to the hearsay rule and argued the testimony showed Amber's intent, plan, and motive.

Judge Foster agreed the testimony met the hearsay rule exception. I thought I had won the argument since there was no way the testimony could be ruled not relevant. I was wrong. Polk argued that Amber's statement to Olivia was made after she had pleaded true to negligent homicide and received her sentence.

Judge Foster said the issue before the court was what actions, if any, Riley took in relation to Davis's commission of her negligent homicide as well as Riley's intention in taking those actions. Miss Davis's intentions were irrelevant in this trial.

I was beside myself. I raised my voice. "Judge, Olivia Turner will testify that Amber Davis never mentioned that Hope Riley was present, much less mention that Hope Riley nodded, intending for Davis to shoot and kill Henry Esposito."

"You can take that up on appeal, Ms. Sanchez. After I seat the jury, call your next witness."

I noticed I was still shaking my head. I had counted on Olivia Turner undermining Amber's testimony. I was now left with calling Hope and trying to explain why she didn't remember what happened at Henry Esposito's apartment until she heard Amber's first shot.

I had spent hours over many months trying to convince Hope that she had been Henry Esposito's victim. She never budged, and after Amber's testimony, many jurors saw Hope as the seducer. When I put her on the stand, I planned to not focus her testimony on being a victim. Instead, I wanted her to convince the jury that Henry Esposito was the key to her potential career. Each day of the trial, Hope had worn pastel skirts or dresses and high-necked blouses. Today, I wanted her to look less innocent and more like a pretty teenage girl.

"The defense calls Hope Riley."

Hope got up from her chair and walked slowly to the witness chair. Sadly, she had lost the vibrant fresh look she had when I first met her.

After taking the oath, Hope sat and looked over at the jury.

I began asking her background questions. Hope told the jury her father had left her mother before she was born and she had never met him. She described the apartment where she and her mother lived.

I asked where she went to school, and Hope told the jury she had been selected to go to the Dallas School for the Performing and Visual Arts. She told the jury she was a singer and acted in plays and wanted also to become a model.

I asked the court permission to show a video of Hope performing in a musical. Polk objected that it wasn't relevant, and Judge Foster decided the jury could see the video. I had taken time reviewing videos taken of Hope to find the snippet I wanted the jury to see. In addition to showing Hope was a talented and gifted young teenager, I wanted the jury to see Hope before she spent over a year in Dallas County Jail. I saw jurors look from the video to Hope in the witness chair and I took that to mean they noticed the difference.

I then turned to her meeting Henry Esposito and what happened afterward. At this point, at least some jurors thought Hope had seduced Henry Esposito when she was fifteen. I thought that was a crazy notion. Henry Esposito had groomed Hope. He had started by building her trust. He quickly understood what Hope wanted and needed at that time and he provided it.

"Hope, when did you meet Henry Esposito?"

"I met Mr. Esposito at our school's talent show. He was one of the judges."

"Tell the jury what happened."

"For that talent show, I sang 'Hallelujah,' and I won first place."

Hope went on to tell the jury that after the talent show, Henry Esposito approached her and asked for any videos and photos she or the school had created of her singing, acting, or modeling. She related that Esposito had said she could become the next Britney Spears. Hope laughed that the example he had given was twenty years earlier. When she laughed, Esposito said he purposely used that example because the teen stars today wanted a punk look that he did not like.

I asked when she next saw Henry Esposito. Hope testified he invited her to a professional photographer, who created a model's portfolio for her. He introduced her to a record producer and to a friend of his who was producing a movie in Dallas and would be able to give her a small part.

Polk objected once again, claiming all of this was irrelevant. I looked over at the jury and I saw several members leaning forward in their chairs, which I took to mean they were interested and wanted to learn more. I responded by telling Judge Foster that if this testimony was irrelevant then everything Darla Esposito and Amber Davis had told the jury about Hope and Henry Esposito was irrelevant. Judge Foster ruled in my favor, and I continued questioning.

Hope told the jury that Henry Esposito became a mentor and took a great interest in her. She described how he asked questions and then listened to her. She said he was the first person who listened to what she was saying. Her mother wanted to listen to her, but she worked two jobs and didn't have time. Hope broke into tears when she told the jury that she wanted to become a star so her mother wouldn't have to work so hard.

"Did Mr. Esposito ask to have sex with you?"

"Yes. That happened about two months after the talent show?"

"Describe what happened."

"Mr. Esposito told me I was the most beautiful young woman he had ever met and asked if he could kiss me. I said yes. The kiss led to other things, and that day he took me into his bedroom. We undressed and he made love to me."

"How old were you at the time?"

"I was fifteen, but I was close to my sixteenth birthday."

"Why did you allow Mr. Esposito to take you into his bedroom and have sex with you?" I asked.

Hope told the jury that after having sex with Henry Esposito, he gave her two hundred dollars. She said he had not paid her to have sex and he gave her that and additional money to buy a new smartphone and smart watch.

Hope said that each time she went to Esposito's apartment, he gave her two hundred dollars. I asked why she accepted the money, and she told the jury that her mother worked two jobs and they still had no money. She also told the jury that when her mother asked, she said she was being paid to model clothes. At least some of the modeling story turned out to be true, but it wasn't modeling clothes.

After a few weeks, he asked if he could take photographs and shoot video of her. At first, he posed her in sexy clothes, holding a gun. Later, he posed her naked, sometimes in heels or boots.

I asked why she had not objected to having sex with Henry Esposito or posing for the sensual photographs and videos.

"I was in high school, where boys my age and older tried to have sex with me the first time we went out together. They repeatedly asked me to send them nude photos. If I said no, they told everyone I was a prude, or worse made up stories about me and shared them online. Mr. Esposito was the opposite. He never did anything with me without asking. He never made fun of me. He never posted anything online. He was a gentleman."

"Did you ever say no?" I asked.

"Yes, Mr. Esposito asked if I would have sex with some of his friends and I told him I did not want to do that. He never asked again."

Hope wanted to convince the jury that Esposito was a good guy. While I knew he wasn't, I wanted her to come across as sincere, and if she persuaded the jurors she loved him, perhaps they would also believe she would not want him to die.

I asked if Henry Esposito asked Hope to pose with his guns.

"Yes. Mr. Esposito had a gun collection and for whatever reason he had a thing for me posing with guns. One time he had me put on black nylons and heels and sit with one leg straight and the other leg bent so I was holding a gun across my chest. I thought it was weird but when I looked at the photo it was sensual looking."

"How often did you see Henry Esposito?" I asked.

"By the time I turned sixteen, Mr. Esposito had gotten an apartment and I saw him every week."

"Did he give you two hundred dollars every week?"

"Yes, by that time, he said it was to help my mother. I also started modeling, for which I was paid, and that helped my mother."

I asked how Amber had gotten involved.

"One day Amber and I were sitting outside at school eating lunch together. My wallet fell out of my purse, and she saw the corners of two one-hundred-dollar bills. She asked where I had gotten that kind of money. I didn't want to tell her, but she pressed me, asking if I was prostituting myself. I said no. To defend myself, I finally told her Mr. Esposito was helping me with my career and giving me money. Amber asked how she could have someone give her that kind of money. I asked Mr. Esposito the next time I saw him, and he told me to bring her to a party he had planned for some friends. We went together."

"Did you and Amber go to other so-called parties together?"

"Yes. We went to several. Several men took an interest in Amber. She demanded and they paid her lots of money."

"What did you do while Amber was engaged with the men."

"I tried to act as a hostess and just be friendly to Mr. Esposito's friends without flirting with any of them."

"Hope, let me take you to the day Amber shot Henry Esposito. Why were the two of you there that day?"

"It was to celebrate my seventeenth birthday. Mr. Esposito asked that I bring Amber."

"Had he asked you to bring Amber before?"

"Yes, once he learned Amber was bisexual, he liked to take photos and videos of us together."

"Are you bisexual?"

"Yes, but I just did it with Amber because it pleased Mr. Esposito."

"So, on the day Amber shot him, how did you get to the apartment?"

"We took Uber. Mr. Esposito had paid on his credit card."

"When you got there, what happened?"

"We celebrated my birthday. He had cake and ice cream."

"Did he give you anything to drink?" I asked.

Hope scrunched her nose, as if trying to remember. "Yes. He gave me a drink, but I cannot tell you what it was."

I asked Hope what happened after the birthday cake, ice cream, and drink. She told the jury Esposito had she and Amber pose in sexy clothes with Amber holding the gun.

"Do you remember approximately what time that was?" I asked.

"I believe it was about two o'clock. We had arrived an hour before."

"What happened after that?"

"I'm sorry, but I don't remember anything until I heard the first shot and came racing in and saw and heard Amber firing the second and third shot as I yelled for her to stop."

Hope had used a phrase she had not told me before. I picked up on that and wanted the jury to do the same.

"Hope, you said you came racing in. Where were you racing in from?"

"It had to be the living room because I remember opening a closed door and racing to where Amber stood with the gun."

"Do you remember the time?" I asked.

"It had to be at least four o'clock because I remember we left at five o'clock."

"Hope, are you wearing a smart watch?" I asked.

I looked over at Polk and she looked puzzled, with her finger on her lip. I expected the first of what would be a series of objections, but she stayed in her seat.

About a week earlier I had finally settled on our best defense. I scolded myself for having not thought about it before. I had asked Hope to let me see her smart watch, which she was allowed to wear to court. I did not want her testimony to be rehearsed, so I didn't tell her why I wanted to see it or what I would ask her about it during her testimony.

"Hope, does your smart watch have a sleep app?"

Polk realized where I was going now and objected and asked for a bench conference. When Judge Foster asked for the grounds for the objection, Polk said I planned to introduce some evidence from the sleep app on Hope's smartphone and there was no evidence what I would introduce would be reliable or had not been manipulated.

I had anticipated the objection, and I had found law review articles writing about the admissibility of data coming from a smartphone or watch. Judge Foster seemed intrigued and wanted to hear more.

I asked Hope to turn her sleep app to November thirtieth of 2019. I had set her watch so she would be able to see what the app recorded for that date. Polk objected again on the same grounds. Judge Foster said I could continue, and by this time, some of the younger jurors knew where I was going with these questions.

Hope testified that her watch reflected she had been asleep from two fifteen to three fifty- five. Polk objected for the third time, but by this time the jurors had all the information they needed.

I asked what happened after Amber shot Esposito.

"We were in a panic. Amber had blood all over her clothes. She said we had to get out of there, go to her home so she could change clothes and run away. I asked why we should run away since she had told me she had shot Mr. Esposito in self-defense. She thought about it and said it really wasn't self-defense. It had been an accident. I asked once again why we should run away if she had accidently shot Mr. Esposito. She said no one would believe us."

"What happened next?"

Hope described them taking Esposito's BMW and driving to Amber's house, where she changed clothes. She said Amber wanted them to drive to Miami. When she asked why Miami, Amber said it was far away and the police would never find them there. Hope testified she asked what they would do for money and Amber said she would take care of that.

"What did Amber do with the gun?" I asked.

"She tossed it out the window on the interstate somewhere east of Dallas."

Hope told jurors about calling her mother, who told her to come home, but Amber had nixed the idea. Then she testified about being caught in Baton Rouge.

"Hope, were you aware when Amber shot Mr. Esposito that he planned to leave you five hundred thousand dollars?"

"No, he had never mentioned it or mentioned dying. I didn't even understand what it meant for me."

"What did you want from Mr. Esposito?"

"I wanted his help getting opportunities for my career. I wanted his guidance. Having a single mom, I had never had a father figure in my life. I know it sounds weird, since he was having sex with me."

"Hope, did you do or say anything to Amber that could possibly have led her to believe you wanted her to pull the trigger?"

"No, when I heard the first shot, I shouted for her to stop, but it was too late."

"When the Baton Rouge police stopped you, they interrogated you for how many hours?"

"I can't remember exactly, but I believe it was three or four hours."

"Why did you tell them that you and Amber shot Esposito?"

"Amber told me that if we ever got caught, we needed to tell the same story. At first, she wanted us to say we shot him in self-defense. The police didn't believe that story. Then we got to talk to each other again and she told me to say it was an accident and she and I didn't know the gun was loaded."

"Was any of that true?"

"No. As I said before, I didn't and still don't remember what happened from the time I finished drinking my soft drink until I heard the first shot."

"And that is what really happened, not what you told the police in Baton Rouge?

"Yes."

I stopped there. Even if jurors thought Hope had seduced Henry Esposito, they could easily conclude she was not even in the same room when Amber fired the first shot. It was one o'clock and I expected Judge Foster to break for lunch. Instead, she told the jury she had other business that afternoon and she excused the jurors until the morning. I thought she was giving Robin Polk both the afternoon and evening to work on her cross-examination. It seemed unfair, but what was I to do?

Chapter 44

Gabriela

The national news media was paying even more attention to our case. Some outlets were disgusted that Robin Polk had tried to make Hope the seducer rather than the victim. They argued that no young teenage girl should be accused of taking advantage of a forty-year-old man,

That night on the cable news networks, they ran video of Hope testifying in what one channel called the "smart watch defense," and another channel called the "sleep app defense."

I received several telephone calls asking me to appear on news shows. I told the callers that Judge Foster had already chastised me for making public statements about the case to the media.

I pondered what Robin Polk would do on cross-examination. I figured her questions would present her theory of the case and make Hope deny each of her points. I told Hope to expect those questions and to answer truthfully as she had done during our direct examination.

The next morning, the courtroom was packed with reporters. After the jury was seated and Hope had resumed her seat in the witness chair, Judge Foster said, "Ms. Polk you may cross-examine the witness."

She started with the last will that Henry Esposito drafted.

"Ms. Riley, isn't it true that you are named as a beneficiary of Henry Esposito's handwritten last will."

I could see Hope wasn't sure how to answer. After pausing, she finally answered, "I am not sure what a beneficiary means."

"You were supposed to receive five hundred thousand dollars in the handwritten will Henry Esposito prepared, isn't that true?

"Yes. I've been told Mr. Esposit—"

Polk interrupted. "You've answered my question."

I asked Judge Foster to allow Hope to finish her answer. Judge Foster agreed.

Hope continued, "Mr. Esposito wanted me to receive five hundred thousand dollars, but I didn't know it when he was alive. I first learned that he wanted me to have the money when my lawyer told me his ex-wife was contesting the handwritten will. That was after he passed away."

"With the money, you'd be able to continue paying for the professionals Mr. Esposito had hired to help you develop your singing, acting, and modeling future, isn't that true?"

"It may be true," Hope responded. "But I told Ms. Sanchez that I didn't want to fight Ms. Esposito to get the money. Mr. Esposito had given me far more than money and I didn't want to fight over the money he left me in his will."

Score one for Hope. Her answers had pretty much eliminated Polk's theory of a motive for Hope to want Henry Esposito dead.

Then Polk turned to the changing stories about what happened.

"Isn't it true you told your mother that you and Amber had shot Henry Esposito."

"Yes." Hope answered.

"Isn't that also what you told the Baton Rouge police in the video we've played for the jurors?"

"Yes."

"And each time you changed your story to the police, there was one thing that did not change and that was that you and Amber together had shot Henry Esposito, right?"

"Yes that is what I told them in the video but it wasn't true."

Polk then violated one of the cardinal rules of cross-examination. Given her experience and reputation, her next question took me by surprise.

"If you were in the other room when you heard the first shot, why did you say you had both shot Mr. Esposito?"

"Because Amber told me she needed me to say she had shot Mr. Esposito in self-defense. Then she decided she needed me to say she had accidently shot Mr. Esposito. I agreed to lie to protect her."

Polk then turned to the two of them stealing Esposito's car and driving to Miami. Hope testified both had been Amber's idea and she went along with the ideas because Amber had convinced her no one would believe their story. She added that after speaking to her mother, she had wanted to return to Dallas and Amber was determined to keep driving to Miami.

Polk asked about another possible motive.

"You wanted Henry Esposito to yourself, didn't you?"

"Yes. I loved Mr. Esposito. He was the first grown person other than my mother who listened to me and tried to understand and help me."

"But he was having sex with other girls, including your friend Amber, isn't that true?"

"Yes. that is true."

"And that made you unhappy, didn't it?"

"Yes. I didn't like it, and I told Mr. Esposito."

"And he continued, including on your birthday?"

"Yes. Mr. Esposito continued, and on my birthday, he wanted to have sex with Amber."

"And that made you mad, didn't it?"

"I wasn't mad. I was disappointed. But you are missing the point. Mr. Esposito was helping me with my career. That was more important to me. He gave me a future. Now I have nothing."

When cross-examining the defendant, the prosecutor wants to end on a high note. Robin Polk couldn't find a question that would end her questions for Hope on a high note. So, after asking a few more questions, she sat down.

"Your Honor, the defense rests," I said while staring at the jurors.

I heard that Robin Polk had had a junior lawyer in her office search for a forensic expert in the hope the expert could testify that the data on a smart watch could be altered or added after the fact. Apparently, the young lawyer failed to find an expert who was willing to testify.

I hoped I had found Hope's best defense.

After we argued over instructions to the jury, Judge Foster asked Polk to deliver her final argument. She, as the prosecutor, would get two chances to persuade the jury, so I had to listen to her first argument and anticipate her second one.

After taking time to thank the jury for their service and paying close attention to the evidence. She started where she had begun in the opening statement.

"Ladies and gentlemen, I told you in the opening statement that this case was relatively simple in that you don't have to figure out who shot and killed Henry Esposito. You only need to decide whether it was murder. Based on the evidence, we know that Amber Davis and the defendant shot and killed Henry Esposito, fled the scene, went home and changed clothes, and started driving his car to Miami. We know that when they were caught in Baton Rouge and given their right to have a lawyer present, they both volunteered to tell the police what happened. Even though they told more than one version of what happened, the one thing that didn't change was they had shot and killed Henry Esposito and fled the scene. If the shooting was in self-defense or was an accident, they could've called the police and let them know about the self-defense or accidental shooting. They didn't. They drove away.

"Even if the defendant did not fire the weapon that killed Henry Esposito. Judge Foster will instruct you that under the law in Texas, when someone is killed during the commission of a felony, a defendant is guilty of murder if she participated in the felony crime. In this case, the crime was the girls robbed Henry Esposito, took his money and his BMW car and left the scene of the crime."

With that, Polk concluded her first final argument, asking the jury to find the defendant guilty of murder.

I focused my argument on Hope's lack of motive and what her watch told jurors.

"Ladies and gentlemen of the jury, Hope Riley had no motive or reason to kill Henry Esposito. He had helped her start her singing, modeling, and movie career. If she killed him, that all stops. The prosecutor has suggested that Hope wanted Henry Esposito to die so she could inherit five hundred thousand dollars. That indeed is a lot of money. But the evidence before you is that Hope didn't even know about this change to his will, and when she learned about it after his death, she chose not to fight Mrs. Esposito to get it."

I turned to the watch defense. I purposely started by telling the jury that Hope was not an accomplice to Amber's shooting Henry Esposito. I continued with the watch defense.

"The best evidence you have of what Hope experienced the day Amber Davis shot Henry Esposito can be found on Hope's watch. Henry Esposito gave Hope a drink. It made her sleepy and affected her memory. Her watch sleep app shows she was asleep when Amber fired the first shot."

I put the gun drawings on the screen again. "The evidence shows that Amber Davis moved the safety on the gun. Then she pulled the slide to the rearmost position to chamber a bullet. Then she pulled the trigger and the bullet struck Henry Esposito. Hope woke up from the noise of the shot and stormed into the bedroom only to find Amber pulling the trigger of the gun again and then again. Hope shouted at Amber to stop, and finally, after putting three bullets into Henry Esposito, Amber stopped."

I paused and looked at each juror. I thought I had reached them.

I told the jury that Hope wanted to report what happened and Amber wanted to drive to Miami. After talking to her mother, Hope asked Amber to go back to Dallas and tell the police what happened. Amber once again chose to keep driving.

"Ladies and gentlemen, Hope Riley is innocent. Her watch proves she was not awake when Amber first fired the weapon. Her life and her future are now in her hands. Let her continue to shine and make a rewarding future."

Polk focused on the watch in her final closing. She told the jury that there was no evidence that what was on the watch was accurate and no evidence suggesting that the defendant could not have manipulated what was presented in court. She asked the jury to consider that the sleep app watch defense was sprung on them at the last minute.

But, as I anticipated, Polk focused on the jury instruction she knew Judge Foster would give.

"Ladies and gentlemen, you don't even have to consider whether the defendant was asleep in the other room when her friend started firing the weapon that killed Henry Esposito. Judge Foster will tell you that the law in Texas is: 'All traditional distinctions between accomplices and principals are abolished…and each party to an offense may be charged and convicted without alleging that he acted as a principal or accomplice.' In this case, the defendant was an accomplice, and it doesn't matter that she was in the other room. She could have been waiting out in Henry Esposito's BMW and still be convicted of his murder."

That instruction hurt us, but its wording was a bit confusing. I wanted the jury to disregard the instruction.

Polk concluded where she had started.

"Ladies and gentlemen, I repeat what I've said before. This case is not complicated. Two girls shot Henry Esposito, stole money from his wallet, stole his BMW, and started driving to Miami. We know who those girls were. One was Amber Davis, and the other was the defendant. They both are guilty regardless of which one pulled the trigger. The defendant and her friend took a father away from his children. You must find the defendant guilty of murder."

Judge Foster instructed the jury, including the felony murder instruction, which didn't require Hope to pull the trigger for them to find her guilty of murder. They retired to the jury room to consider their verdict. Hope and I stayed in the courthouse until the jury quit deliberating that day.

We came back the next day and waited, but no verdict came that day either. I was getting worried. During the afternoon, the jury sent a question to Judge Foster. Their question scared me.

"Can the defendant be found guilty even if she had no idea her friend would shoot Henry Esposito?"

After hearing my argument that Hope was in Mr. Esposito's apartment to celebrate her birthday—she wasn't even in the room when Amber Davis took a loaded weapon and fired the first shot that struck Henry Esposito—Robin Polk suggested that the defendant could have anticipated that Amber Davis would shoot Henry Esposito.

Judge Foster didn't buy Polk's argument. She told the jury they should scrutinize what Hope did after the shooting to determine whether she acted in a way that was consistent with an innocent person or a guilty person.

I thought what Judge Foster told the jury would work in our favor since she did many things after the shooting that were consistent with an innocent person.

I feel more stress waiting for juries to return verdicts than any other part of my work. I can't do anything other than wait, This time, I couldn't eat. I couldn't sleep. I had no work to do. I couldn't go to the office. Long ago, I decided going to the office while waiting for a jury verdict was bad luck. I spent the day with Hope. There was nothing we could do, so we sat and didn't say very much to each other. All I could do was assure her that if the jury had wanted to find her guilty, they could have done that in a matter of hours.

On the third day at noon, the jury announced they had reached a verdict. The media gathered outside the courthouse. Hope and I walked from the witness room where we had waited each day.

Knowing the media was following the case, Judge Foster made the jury decision as dramatic as she could. That meant we all had more time to speculate what the jury had found.

When they walked into the courtroom, I looked to see if any jurors looked at Hope. When jurors don't look at the defendant, it is never a good sign. I saw two jurors look at her. They didn't smile, but I took their expression to be a positive sign.

Hope and I stood as the jury foreman read not guilty to each of the charges. Hope cried and collapsed in my arms. I wasn't sure I could hold her up, but after about thirty seconds, she raised her head and hugged me.

For the first time in eighteen months, Hope was free to go home, But the damage had been done to her. While she had avoided COVID, she had been isolated. She had gone months without seeing her mother, and she had spent days alone and bored in her small cell.

As I walked out of the courtroom, Daniel stopped me.

"Well done," he said. "Now that our conflict is over, do you want to go out with me tonight to celebrate?"

I still didn't know if Daniel was among Henry Esposito's friends who had abused teenage girls. I thanked him for asking, but I told him I had moved on. I hadn't found anyone else, but I didn't want to be with him.

That night I received two telephone calls. The first was from a Rio Grande Valley priest. He told me a twenty-three-year-old woman who had been trafficked when she was a teenager was charged with trafficking a fifteen-year-old girl. The second call was from Congressman Moreno. He told me it was time to start planning for my run for his congressional seat.

Epilogue

A few months after the trial, my phone rang. I recognized the caller's number. It was William Scott, the true-crime writer.

"Do you want to hear what really happened to Henry Esposito?" he asked.

"Does it really matter now?" I replied.

"Aren't you at least a little curious?"

"Sure, tell me what you plan to publish."

"What I am about to tell you would sell a million books and would be a hit on the Investigation Discovery channel. But my publisher's attorneys will not let them publish what I have uncovered."

"Okay, tell me what would make the true crime top-selling book I will never get a chance to read." I was curious how he had learned what happened.

"There were many people who wanted Henry Esposito dead. The first was Darla Esposito, who stood to receive five million dollars in insurance money. The second was Henry Esposito himself who was about to be charged with trafficking teenage girls. Beyond the Espositos, each of Henry's pals who were exploiting underage girls didn't want to be caught in Henry's web."

That all made sense to me, but none of it explained the connection to Amber, who pulled the trigger.

"For Darla to receive the insurance money, Henry's death could not be by suicide," I said.

"Yes, Darla and Henry both knew it. A month before his death, Darla started using neuro-linguistic programming and hypnotism to persuade Henry Esposito to always keep a loaded gun by his side and to give it to Amber Davis to fire."

"How do you know that?" I asked.

"I have my sources," Scott replied.

This all seemed farfetched to me, but I was curious.

"Shortly before Henry's death, Darla met with Amber and offered to pay her one hundred thousand dollars if she shot and killed Henry. To earn the money, Amber had to kill Henry and take Hope with her to Miami. Once in Miami, Darla would wire the funds."

I started laughing. "No wonder your publisher stopped you from publishing your book. You are making this up. Among other things, there are too many parts that must synch together."

"You can laugh all you want, but while you are laughing and thinking I made this up, didn't you ask yourself why Amber wanted to go to Miami and why she insisted that Hope go with her?"

I admitted that never made sense to me.

"Darla put together a plan and Amber was all in. Was Hope part of it?"

"Henry wanted to make sure Hope was not in the room when Amber shot him so he put a magic formula in Hope's soft drink that he knew would cause her to fall asleep and not remember what happened. He thought Amber would be charged with murdering him and Hope would not be. He didn't care about Amber."

"Okay, so explain to me why Amber never pointed a finger in Darla's direction."

"It was the hundred thousand dollars. That was always on the table if Amber kept her mouth shut. Mark my words, as soon as Amber is released from juvenile detention, you'll be able to track her down in Miami and she'll have one hundred thousand dollars."

"If Darla gives her the money, Amber will have no reason to keep quiet."

"I understand Darla plans to pay Amber each year so there is an incentive to keep quiet."

"Wow, that is a wild story," I said.

"Not really a wild story. You had to wonder why Amber shot him. Darla wanted Esposito to die, and he wanted to commit suicide. She couldn't let him do that, so she made the offer to Amber and that set it all in motion."

"The one flaw in Henry Esposito's plan was not thinking Hope would be charged with murder."

"Oh, I think Darla included that in her plan. That was why Amber testified against Hope. There was a little revenge motive there. Oh, and there is one more thing I found doing research for the book."

"What's that?"

"I also uncovered the names of Esposito's friends who were most likely engaging in sex with minors."

Scott anticipated my question.

"Neither Daniel Thompson nor Christopher Duval were among the names I uncovered."

"That is good to know," I replied.

A few weeks later, after finishing a morning run, I settled in my chair with my coffee and opened my iPad to my news app. I was stunned when I read an article about the top athletes in the world who were dealing with mental health concerns. For many, this was the first time they had ever made public the challenges they were facing. Over the next few weeks, several other top athletes acknowledged the stress they were under.

I understood. I had spent my career successfully dealing with the stress to win whatever case I was trying. Even when I defended Sparks Duval and my career depended on winning, I dealt with the stress once the trial started.

This time it was different. I don't know if it was because I was defending a teenager whose future depended on me or because COVID had delayed the trial so many times and left me home alone, but something was different. Like my father before me, I had turned to alcohol. I didn't like it, but I did it anyway.

I pondered my future. I could go back home and run for Congress in 2022 or I could stay in Dallas and convince myself that my drinking was because of the stress from the case, not because I would feel that way again.

After Hope's defense, I appeared on local and national television shows explaining the "smart watch" defense. I received praise for my brilliance, but the media did not know I was troubled.

Many supposedly brilliant trial lawyers are less brilliant than perceived and win their cases by their thorough preparation and knowledge of all the relevant facts. The "smart watch" defense was in front of me from the day I first met Hope, but it eluded me until something clicked during the trial. What if nothing had clicked? Would Hope be headed off to a long prison sentence?

I had never tried a case with more stress and anxiety. I was sure the COVID delays contributed to it. But, more than anything, I had a teenage girl's life in my hands. Like Simone Biles, I had trouble visualizing my success. I told God that if he would somehow help me successfully defend Hope, I would never tempt fate again.

I finished my coffee and started my morning run, determined to slow down and eventually go home and run for Congress.

www.ingramcontent.com/pod-product-compliance
Lightning Source LLC
Chambersburg PA
CBHW041134110526
44590CB00027B/4015